Adventure Travel in Latin America

Adventure Travel in Latin America

Where to Backpack, Camp and Find Adventure in Mexico, the Caribbean, Central America and South America

Scott Graham

WILDERNESS PRESS
Berkeley, California

FIRST EDITION 1990
2nd printing May 1991
Copyright © 1990 by Scott Graham
Cover photos by Scott Graham and Kevin Graham
Cover design by Larry Van Dyke
Book design by Roslyn Bullas
Library of Congress Catalog Number 90-37146
International Standard Book Number 0-89997-105-9

Manufactured in the United States of America

Published by   Wilderness Press
               2440 Bancroft Way
               Berkeley, CA 94704
               (415) 843-8080
               Write for free catalog

Front cover photos (clockwise from top): Cordillera Real, Bolivia; Macchu Picchu, Peru; Peruvian children near Lake Titicaca; Iguazu Falls, Argentina and Brazil
Back cover photos (top to bottom): Huayna Potosi, Cordillera Real, Bolivia; Agua Azul, Chiapas, Mexico; Takesi Trail, Cordillera Real, Bolivia

Library of Congress Cataloging in Publication Data

Graham, Scott.
   Adventure travel in Latin America : where to backpack, camp, and find adventure in Mexico, the Caribbean, Central America, and South America / by Scott Graham. — 1st ed.
      p.   cm.
   Includes bibliographical references and index.
   ISBN 0-89997-105-9 (paper)
      1. Latin America—Description and travel—1981- —Guide-books. 2. Backpacking—Latin America—Guide-books. 3. Camping—Latin America—Guide-books. 4. Outdoor recreation—Latin America—Guide-books. I. Title.
F1408.29.G7   1990
918'.0438—dc20   90-37146
                                                        CIP

In memory of Pamela Lee,
whose selfless, untamed spirit will be with us always.

Contents

Chapter 1

Why This Book Exists and How to Use It

Leo Le Bon co-founded Mountain Travel with two friends in the 1960s to take adventurous tourists where most Westerners had never before trodden. Today, more than 20 years later, citizens of the industrialized world spend millions of dollars each year on adventure travel. As groups or individuals, more Westerners are exploring backcountry areas of the developing world—often called the Third World—than ever before. They're bushwhacking through steaming jungles, riding camels across blazing deserts and climbing the flanks of glacier-clad peaks. With many developing countries becoming increasingly open to travelers, and with the cost of international airfares steadily decreasing in real dollars, the number of travelers venturing into the developing world's backcountry areas is rapidly growing.

Those undertaking such journeys have learned that by being even slightly adventurous—by leaving "civilization" behind for a few days or weeks—they can experience some of the hospitality and depth of culture possessed by the peoples of the developing world. At the same time, they experience the joy and challenge of any journey in the outdoors.

Why Latin America?

For several reasons, Latin America is at the top of many Westerners' lists of places they'd most like to visit.

Westerners can travel to Latin America simply, quickly and affordably. Many parts of Mexico's backcountry are an easy, safe automobile drive from Canada and the United States. Inexpensive flights to the Caribbean from Europe and North America have been available for many years. More recently, inexpensive flights to many Central and South American cities have been popping up on travel agents' computer screens. Since the mid-1980s, the cost of flying to Central and South America has fallen dramatically. Today, most flights from Europe and North America to Central and South America approximate the cost per mile of flights within Europe and North America. In Central or South America, the strength of the dollar and other hard currencies compared to local currencies often makes the price of in-country and country-to-country flights even less expensive.

Another reason for Latin America's popularity as an adventure-travel destination is that the cost of living in Latin American countries is extremely inexpensive by industrialized-world standards. Decent hotel rooms may be rented for a few dollars a night; delicious meals may range in price from fifty cents to a dollar.

Even more important to the adventure traveler, Latin America's countries offer a wealth of backcountry travel experiences, from sea kayaking and river rafting to mountain climbing, backpacking and bicycling. All this is available at minimal cost only a few hours by plane from virtually any city in North America and Europe. As a *Summit* magazine article on climbing Huascaran, the highest mountain in Peru, pointed out, "You can leave your Los Angeles office at 5 p.m. Friday, have breakfast in Lima, and dine at the base of Huascaran on Saturday night."

Perhaps the best reason to travel to Latin America is to meet the fascinating people of the region. While English, Portuguese and various Indian languages are spoken in some parts of Latin America, Spanish is the predominant language of the region. Hence little more than a scant grasp of Spanish, or the willingness to make steady use of a Spanish-English dictionary, enables backcountry travelers in Latin America to enjoy the company of some of the earth's friendliest people—Latin Americans.

Leaving Roads Behind

Maybe you're curious about so-called adventure travel, but are not aware of the many backcountry journeys that you can undertake as a member of a group or on your own in Latin America. If so, this book should help you decide if you want to spend your next vacation traveling through the backcountry of some exciting Latin locale.

Many Westerners are electing to add a dose of excitement to their next vacation by journeying in the developing world's backcountry. For them, the questions are where to go, and what to do when they get there. This book is designed to help with those decisions. Its pages contain information on the many backcountry adventure opportunities Latin America offers. You have only to read, and to choose.

Mountain Travel's Le Bon decided more than two decades ago he wanted to do it all. In the last quarter century, he has very nearly done so. Today, Le Bon is known as the father of adventure travel. He is undeniably adventure travel's most ardent supporter. *Outside* magazine ran an article on Le Bon in the late 1980s. "You've got to get away from the roads," the indefatigable backcountry traveler told his interviewer. "That's essential."

And that, essentially, is adventure travel: getting away from roads, far from the comforts—and confines—of the industrialized world.

My wife, Sue, and I strongly believe in leaving roads as far behind as possible when we travel. While we haven't traveled the globe to the extent Le Bon has, we *have* traveled through many backcountry areas of Latin America and other parts of the developing world. As a result, we are often asked for advice by friends considering similar journeys. Like us, those we talk to usually want to explore intriguing areas of the world not yet teeming with tourists. Invariably, we find ourselves recommending Latin America because it is affordable and easy to get to, its adventure-travel possibilities are nonpareil, and its people are friendly and hospitable. This book grew out of our private Latin American travel recommendations. It exists to help you decide whether to undertake an adventure-travel journey to Latin America, and if so, where to go and what to do on your journey.

It would be impossible to visit every area, trail, beach, river and mountain mentioned in this book. In that respect, this book is unlike a detailed guidebook whose author has visited each place described therein. Rather, this book contains information on Latin American countries and their backcountry opportunities that will let you decide what interests you and what does not.

The description of each country in this book is divided into five parts. An overview provides general information about the country, including a brief history. Sections on the country's geography and climate follow. Next, adventure-travel possibilities in the country are described. The possibilities are numbered to correspond with the location numbers on each country map. Last, an "information sources" section discusses guidebooks and other information on the country, emphasizing information helpful to backcountry travelers.

Of Special Note

It is important to note that some of the guidebooks listed in this book are fairly obscure or are out of print. You may be unable to locate a book you want in your local library or bookstore. If so, you can order the book directly from its publisher or through a bookstore, or you can take advantage of the inter-library loan program available at most public libraries.

As you read this book, you'll note some of the major environmental problems confronting Latin American countries are mentioned. Westerners fight to preserve wilderness in their countries because they are aware of the need to protect their wilderness. Similarly, I hope visitors to Latin America will begin to work to protect the rights of the peoples and animals of Latin America's backcountry areas—if they're aware of those areas' problems and needs. And the best way for them to become aware is to travel in those fascinating areas. Only during such journeys can travelers learn first hand of the fragility of Latin America's backcountry and the need for its protection.

This book celebrates adventure travel. It describes the many opportunities awaiting adventurous travelers in backcountry areas of Latin America, and it encourages the minimum-impact exploration of those areas.

Chapter 2

An Overview of Latin America

From quiet Caribbean coves to rugged Andean peaks, Latin America offers physical attractions for every backcountry enthusiast. On top of that are the incomparable people of Latin America's backcountry areas. The centuries-old cultures of those people—cultures still relatively intact in the backcountry—make adventure travel in Latin America especially intriguing. However, the modern-day politics of the region combined with the growing influence of the cocaine trade in some parts of South America makes many Westerners wary of traveling in Latin America.

It is an unfortunate fact that civil wars and guerrilla movements made travel unsafe for North Americans in a few Latin American countries in the 1980s. The 1990s have begun with more of the same. However, just as plenty of areas in Latin America were open and entirely safe for backcountry travelers throughout the 1980s, so will plenty of areas remain or become open to travelers in the years ahead.

This book provides an overview of the political climate of each Latin American country. However, the best way for you to determine the safety and stability of the country or countries you wish to visit is to study the international pages of a large metropolitan newspaper before you leave. If all is quiet in the area you plan to visit, it will most likely remain so during your journey. If trouble is brewing, you may be wise to change your plans.

The Debt Crisis and Its Implications

The Latin American debt crisis had its origin in the 1970s, when Latin American countries began accepting loans from the world's largest private financial institutions. The money was to be used to start profitable businesses that would contribute to the local economy and help repay the loans. When the loans were made, the lending institutions were flush with Mideast oil money.

"With the easy availability of credit, discipline on the part of borrowers and lenders eroded," Sarah Bartlett wrote in the *New York Times*. "In the end, much of the [more than $400 billion Latin American] debt incurred in the 1970s was not used to build factories or to purchase new equipment, efforts that would have supported new economic activity and generated income to pay off the debt."

The money was quickly gone, leaving only the need for the loans to be repaid. Today, the debtor countries are in bad financial shape. Most of the debtor countries—Mexico, Argentina and Brazil owe the most—are barely paying the interest they owe each year, and are making no headway on the principal. The countries are desperate for hard currency with which to pay off their loans. As a result, they have turned a hungry eye on their natural resources. Lumbering and mining efforts have been stepped up without regard for the environment, and social welfare programs have been scaled back or discontinued.

What do the debt crisis and its effects mean to Westerners considering travel in Latin America? Plenty.

As Latin American countries struggle to pay off their debts, fragile backcountry areas throughout the region are coming under increasing pressure. Since the banks have shown little inclination to forgive the bulk of Latin America's debt, Latin governments are trying to squeeze what hard currency they can from their available natural resources. They are delving deeper and deeper into their backyards for exportable resources. In Brazil, lumbering for hardwoods and slash-and-burn practices by landless settlers are bringing about the destruction of the Amazon basin's rain forests at a frightening rate. The bare soil uncovered by such methods— usually only a few inches deep, since most of a rain forest's life is in its treetops—is washed away by heavy seasonal rains, leaving unproductive wasteland. In both Central and South America, wide swaths of forest are being slashed and burned to make room for cattle ranching to produce beef for export to the industrialized world.

In a small way, your journeying to the backcountry of Latin America can help bring about an end to these rapacious practices. Your journey can help preserve the backcountry for the peoples of

Latin America who have lived there for centuries because, as a visitor, you'll be spending the hard currency Latin American countries desperately need to repay their loans. If backcountry tourism in Latin America becomes a large enough business, the money it takes in will more than offset the quick profits governments can make by destroying their forests. Then, those governments will take action to curb deforestation.

A Little History

Before the arrival of the Spanish conquistadors in the 16th century, Latin America was a land of many native groups whose different lifestyles were uniquely adapted to their different homelands, from the island peoples of the Caribbean to the hardy peoples of the high Andes.

The Aztec, Mayan and Incan civilizations interest modern travelers to Latin America because of the impressive ruins that survive from the years of their eminence. The Aztec civilization was based in what is now central Mexico. The Mayan civilization spread throughout northern Central America and southern Mexico. The capital of the far-reaching Incan empire was the city of Cuzco, in southern Peru. From Cuzco, an amazing system of stone-paved footpaths stretched for thousands of miles through the Andes to the far reaches of the empire in what are now Bolivia, Chile, Argentina and Ecuador. Today, the remnants of those paths offer paved-trail hiking, with convenient stairways at steep points, through rugged backcountry areas offering some of the most beautiful mountain scenery in the world. The most famous stretch of the remaining Inca road system is the Inca Trail, which links Cuzco with the ancient city of Machu Picchu, the mysterious Incan spiritual center lying astride a mountain saddle high above the Urubamba River.

The arrival of the conquistadors from Spain in the early 1500s brought an end to the many wealthy, advanced indigenous civilizations of Latin America that had grown, warred, flourished and faltered until then. While the Portuguese set up colonization in Brazil, and other European nations, including Spain, did the same in the Caribbean, various Spanish conquistadors busied themselves taking as much gold and silver as they could out of the rest of Mexico, Central America and South America. The booty obtained by the conquistadors was shipped to Spain, where it funded wars waged by Spain in its failed attempt to gain superiority in Europe.

Soon after the conquistadors came Spanish emissaries of the Catholic Church, seeking to replace Latin America's many indigenous religions with Catholicism. In one sense, they did a good job—Latin America is today a land of Catholics. In many areas, however, that Catholicism is little more than a framework within which Latin Americans continue to practice their indigenous religions. Indian religious festivals in the Andes feature gods and goddesses as different from Jesus and the Virgin Mary as water is from wine, while voodoo and witchcraft still permeate the societies of former African slaves throughout the Caribbean.

For their part, the conquistadors and the colonial governors from Spain who followed did their jobs well. Through a system of ruthless control, they took all they could from Latin America, first in forcibly-mined precious metals, then in forcibly-grown cash crops. In the 1800s, Spain's influence in Central America and northern South America gave way to that of the United States, which set up a series of "banana republics" in the region. Profits from cash crops in the region were simply exported north, rather than across the Atlantic to the Iberian peninsula.

More than 400 years of steady exploitation have left much of Latin America undereducated, woefully poor and little prepared for self-governance. Still, Latin Americans treat visitors with friendliness and kindness. Their zest for life is apparent to visitors at every turn. The industrialized world has done much to destroy Latin America's economic foundations; it is reassuring to learn by visiting that Latin America's soul has not been affected.

What's There to Do?

For the adventure traveler, the best news about Latin America is that, despite centuries of exploitation that continues today, there remain large areas of jungle, desert and mountains that are little explored and tremendously beautiful. The means for visiting those areas are nearly as varied as the areas themselves, whether travelers choose to travel on their own or with group tours. Several Latin American countries—Mexico, Belize, Costa Rica, Ecuador, Brazil, Chile and Argentina—offer good opportunities for first-time, do-it-yourself adventure journeys. For experienced travelers, backcountry adventures await in virtually every Latin American country. For those thinking of joining organized tours, many agencies offer adventure-travel tours in Latin America. Those agencies are described and listed in the following chapter.

The two natural features that most determine the adventure travel possibilities in Latin America are the region's generally tropical climate, and the mountain ranges and volcanoes that run through central Mexico, down the spine of Central America and along the western edge of South America.

The climate of much of Latin America is tropical, including virtually all the low-lying areas—the islands of the Caribbean, most of the Central and South American coastlines, the jungle regions of the Amazon basin, and other low-lying regions of South America's interior. The equator passes through northern South America. Only the coastlines of Argentina and Chile, which are far south of the equator, and the Peruvian coastline, which is cooled by the Pacific Ocean's Humboldt current, cannot be considered tropical.

Latin America's warm coasts and interior areas make possible a wide range of tropical adventure opportunities. These include river rafting, jungle treks to ancient ruins and secluded beaches, snorkeling and scuba diving, fishing, sea kayaking, canoeing, traveling by hired boat in swamps and along jungle waterways— as well as lying on the beach soaking up some February sunshine.

The mountains of Latin America offer a far different, but no less varied, range of possibilities. Beginning mountaineers can test themselves on glacier-clad volcanoes near Mexico City that rise to 18,000 feet (5,500 meters), and on snow- and ice-covered Andean peaks in South America that require a minimum of technical skills and rise above 20,000 feet (6,000 meters). The Andes also offer an array of highly technical climbs for more experienced climbers. Non-technical, walk-up peaks are found everywhere in Latin America, from Jamaica and the volcanoes of Central America to the southern reaches of Chile and Argentina.

Latin America's mountains offer many backpacking and day hiking possibilities. Copper Canyon—known as the Grand Canyon of Mexico—is located in the Sierra Madre. The heavily forested spine of Central America offers countless possibilities for foot-propelled travelers. Surviving sections of the Inca road system may be hiked in Ecuador, Peru and Bolivia. And the Lake District, straddling the Andes of southern Argentina and Chile, offers hiking through a region that is often compared to the Alps. Other sports, too, may be enjoyed in the mountains. Kayaking and rafting are popular on several Andean rivers, and ski areas abound in the Lake District.

Chapter 3

Adventure-Travel Agencies and General Information Sources

Agencies in the industrialized world and Latin America have offered adventure-travel tours in Latin American countries since the birth of the adventure-travel industry in the 1960s. In recent years, the number of agencies and the scope of their offerings have increased in response to Westerners' growing interest in backcountry vacations.

A solid core of adventure-travel agencies like Mountain Travel, Wilderness Travel and Himalayan Travel have been in business many years. They offer top-notch tours, and charge top-notch prices. Smaller agencies offer comparable trips to Latin America, often at prices far less than those of the larger agencies. Some agencies grow rapidly in size and scope, only to go out of business months later. Others stay in business as small operations, but their cut-rate prices beget cut-rate journeys. Still others offer exceptional tours at exceptional prices. Agencies that fall into all of these categories may be found in the list that follows.

The field of U.S.-based agencies offering organized adventure tours in Latin America is crowded and competitive. As a result, in virtually every instance, you'll receive good value for the money you pay, whether you sign on for a Rolls-Royce tour with the likes of Mountain Travel or for a budget package with a smaller agency.

Some U.S.-Based Agencies Offering Adventure-Travel Tours in Latin America

Above the Clouds Trekking, P.O. Box 398, Worcester, MA 01602. Phone: (800) 233-4499, or (508) 799-4499 in Massachusetts.

Adventure Center, 5540 College Ave., Oakland, CA 94618. Phone: (800) 227-8747, or (415) 654-1879 in California.

The Adventurers' Company, P.O. Box 460224, Houston, TX 77056. Phone: (713) 974-0946.

All Adventure Travel, 7633 Leesburg Pike, Falls Church, VA 22043. Phone: (800) 537-4025, or (703) 556-3434 in Virginia.

Arizona Raft Adventures, 4050 E. Huntington Dr., Flagstaff, AZ 86004. Phone: (602) 526-8200.

Arrow to the Sun Touring, P.O. Box 115, Taylorsville, CA 95983. Phone: (916) 284-6263.

Baja Expeditions, 2625 Garnet Ave., San Diego, CA 92109. Phone: (800) 843-6967, or (619) 581-3311 in California.

Camino Real Tours, 11738 Victory Blvd., North Hollywood, CA 91606. Phone: (800) 626-5285, or (800) 826-3303 in California.

CanoAndes Expeditions, 310 Madison Ave., New York, NY 10017. Phone: (800) 242-5554, or (212) 286-9415 in New York.

Colorado Mountain School Treks and Expeditions, P.O. Box 2062, Estes Park, CO 80517. Phone: (800) 444-0730.

Expeditions, P.O. Box 998, New Canaan, CT 06840. Phone: (800) 888-9400, or (203) 966-2691 in Connecticut.

Explorama Tours, 19 W. 34th St., Suite 700, New York, NY 10001. Phone: (800) 223-6764, or (800) 522-5568 in New York.

Forum Travel International, 91 Gregory Lane, No. 21, Pleasant Hill, CA 94523. Phone: (415) 671-2900.

Genet Expeditions, P.O. Box 230861, Anchorage, AK 99523. Phone: (800) 334-3638, or (907) 561-2123 in Alaska.

Himalayan Travel, P.O. Box 481, Greenwich, CT 06836. Phone: (800) 225-2380, or (203) 622-6777 in Connecticut.

Inca Floats, 1311 63rd St., Emeryville, CA 94608. Phone: (415) 420-1550.

Journeys Unlimited, P.O. Box 16257, Santa Fe, NM 87506. Phone: (505) 471-4494.

Lost World Adventures, 1189 Autumn Ridge Dr., Marietta, GA 30066. Phone: (800) 999-0558.

Mountain Travel, 6420 Fairmont Ave., El Cerrito, CA 94530. Phone: (800) 227-2384, or (415) 527-8100 in California.

Nichols Expeditions, P.O. Box 418, Frisco, CO 80443. Phone: (303) 453-0626.

Overseas Adventure Travel, 349 Broadway, Cambridge, MA 02139. Phone: (800) 221-0814, or (617) 876-0533 in Massachusetts.

Peaks and Places, P.O. Box 622, Avon, CO 81620. Phone: (303) 949-5479.

Pegasus Charters, 530 S.W. 13th Ave., Ft. Lauderdale, FL 33312. Phone: (305) 525-3865.

REI Adventures, P.O. Box 8090, Berkeley, CA 94707. Phone: (800) 622-2236, or (800) 624-2236 in California.

Slickrock Kayak Adventures, P.O. Box 1400, Moab, UT 84532. Phone: (801) 259-6996.

Sobek, P.O. Box 1089, Angels Camp, CA 95222. Phone: (209) 736-4524.

Tropical Adventures, 170 Denny Way, Seattle, WA 98109. Phone: (800) 247-3483.

Turtle Tours, 251 E. 51st St., New York, NY 10022. Phone: (212) 355-1404.

Wilderness Travel, 801 Allston Way, Berkeley, CA 94710. Phone: (800) 247-6700, or (415) 548-0420 in California.

Wildland Journeys, 3516 NE 155th, Seattle, WA 98155. Phone: (800) 345-4453, or (206) 365-0686 in Washington.

Local Agencies

In addition to tour agencies based in industrialized countries, every tourist town and city in Latin America has several locally owned and operated tour agencies. In addition to bus and taxi tours, those local agencies often provide guide services and back-country adventure tours ranging from jungle exploration and river rafting to backpacking and mountain climbing.

The quality of tours provided by local agencies varies widely. However, the price of locally operated tours is a fraction of the price of comparable tours offered by Western agencies. Better still, the leaders of local tours are generally locals rather than Westerners. Finally, unlike tours based in Western countries, all the profits from a locally operated tour remain in the country where the tour takes place.

In most cases, no advance reservations are required for locally operated tours. Upon arrival at a destination, visitors have only to shop around to learn what is available, then join the next scheduled trip.

General Information Sources

Several publications, publishers, book dealers and organizations are worthy of mention as sources of general information concerning adventure travel in Latin America.

For travelers who will be visiting more than one or two Latin American countries, the *South American Handbook*, the *Mexico and Central American Handbook*, and the *Caribbean Islands Handbook* are all highly recommended. They are *the* definitive guides to Latin America. The books are updated annually. They offer brief descriptions of just about everything a visitor might consider seeing or doing in Latin America, and include reports on thousands of restaurants and hotels in Latin America.

The *Handbook* is a prized theft item in Latin America. It is so popular among visitors to Latin America that new copies are virtually impossible to find, and used copies—many undoubtedly stolen—sell for as much as $80 in used book stalls in Latin American cities.

One woman I met in South America was despondent when her copy of the *Handbook* was stolen in northern Peru. She considered flying back to Quito, Ecuador, where she'd seen copies of the book for sale, but convinced herself to forge onward without her "bible." In Lima, she spotted—and quickly purchased—a used copy on sale for $18. "There was that bright red bird looking at me," she told me later, referring to the crimson parrot gracing the book's cover.

For travelers who will be visiting several Latin countries, the *Handbook* is indeed a tremendous help with transportation, hotels and restaurants. The *South American Handbook* mentions many backcountry journeys but contains little detailed information on them, so it is not mentioned elsewhere in this book.

Another guidebook to all of Latin America, **South America on a Shoestring**, published by Lonely Planet Publications, details several backcountry journeys in Latin America. Those descriptions are mentioned where appropriate later in this book.

Lonely Planet Publications (Embarcadero West, 112 Linden St., Oakland, CA 94607) is a leading publisher of guidebooks for the developing world. The first Lonely Planet guides were aimed specifically at travelers visiting the developing world on the cheap. The scope of the company's guides has been expanded over the years to include information for all travelers who want to visit parts of the developing world off the beaten tourist path. In the last few years, Lonely Planet has published several guidebooks for specific South American countries. In this book, they are listed in the "information source" sections of those countries. All of Lonely Planet's guidebooks for South America do an adequate job of listing backcountry travel possibilities.

Since the 1970s, **Bradt Publications** has produced a series of excellent books on backcountry journeys in various parts of Latin America. Those books are mentioned where appropriate later.

The **South American Explorers Club** (P.O. Box 18327, Denver, CO 80218) is an excellent source of information about adventure travel in South America. Members and non-members may order travel books and maps from the club's mail-order catalog. Members receive the club's quarterly newsletter, discounts on mail-order purchases, and use of the organization's clubhouse in Lima, Peru.

Four publications help travelers keep abreast of the latest adventure travel agencies and tours. *Outside* magazine (1165 N. Clark St., Chicago, IL 60610) prints the Expedition Services Directory at the back of each of its monthly issues. The directory is a compilation of classified ads from adventure-travel agencies offering journeys around the world. *Great Expeditions* magazine (P.O. Box 8000-411, Abbotsford, BC V2S 6H1, Canada) offers accounts of adventure-travel journeys intermixed with many adventure-travel-agency advertisements. *Explore* magazine (#470, 301-14th St. NW, Calgary, AB T2N 2A1, Canada) is another Canadian publication focussing on do-it-yourself adventure travel around the globe. The *Unique and Exotic Travel Reporter* newsletter (P.O. Box 98833, Tacoma, WA 98449) provides information on offbeat and adventurous tours.

Going Places: The Guide to the Travel Guides, published by The Harvard Common Press, critically reviews and evaluates more than 3,000 travel guides and series, and includes appendixes listing almost 100 travel bookstores and mail-order outlets, 400 travel publishers and more than 100 travel magazines and other publications.

Several U.S. mail-order book dealers stock hard-to-find guidebooks:

Book Passage, 51 Tamal Vista Blvd., Corte Madera, CA 94925. Phone: (800) 321-9785, or (415) 927-0960 in California.

Chessler Books, P.O. Box 4267, Evergreen, CO 80439. Phone: (800) 654-8502, or (303) 670-0093 in Colorado.

The Complete Traveller, 199 Madison Ave., New York, NY 10016. Phone: (212) 685-9007.

Easy Going, 1400 Shattuck Ave., Berkeley, CA 94709. Phone: (800) 233-3533, or (415) 843-3533 in California.

Chapter 4

A Primer to Adventure Travel

Exploring the backcountry of Latin America and other parts of the developing world differs greatly from backcountry journeys in the industrialized world. Those differences, and how to cope with them, are detailed in my book, *Backpacking and Camping in the Developing World*, published by Wilderness Press. Only the basics are covered here.

If you're a first-time traveler in the developing world, you most likely have plenty of concerns. However, many Westerners travel overseas—by one count, more than ten million every year from only North America. An increasing number of those travelers are journeying in the developing world's backcountry. They've worked out answers to many of your concerns. You need only determine which of the answers best suit your needs.

Awareness

A travel agent I know organized a month-long trek to the base of Mt. Everest for a group of U.S. citizens. Most of the members of the group were accustomed to dealing with tough situations. None, however, had been to the developing world before. Upon their arrival in Kathmandu, and during the days that followed, all reported being deeply shocked by the degree of poverty they saw in Nepal.

"I didn't think it would hit them that hard, considering what they do for a living," my friend told me. "It must really be something over there."

Most of us have seen poverty. We've driven through (or lived in) poor sections of cities, and we've seen the run-down homes of the rural poor. None of that, however, compares with the extreme degree of poverty you'll see in all of the developing world, including Latin America.

All visitors to Latin America come in direct contact with poverty, so it is best to be mentally prepared for it. If the journey to Latin America for which you're preparing will be your first to the developing world, expect to have your senses jangled. Then you may not be so startled by what you see.

In addition to being mentally prepared for poverty, you must also be prepared to be the center of attention for much of your journey. Visitors are rare and hence interesting to locals in the backcountry. In addition, your relative wealth will make you the target of many persistent merchants. Be patient and firm.

You'll also be the target of thieves. Vigilance is the best way to foil thievery. Most thieves in Latin America are opportunists. If you don't give them the opportunity to nab your gear, they'll simply move on to someone less vigilant. Keep all important papers in a pouch beneath your clothes whenever you're out in public.

Money

Although travel in most Latin American countries is remarkably affordable, it isn't free. The best way to carry the money you'll need is by traveler's check. American Express traveler's checks are best because the company has the most overseas offices for replacing stolen checks, and check users may use the mail-holding service offered by American Express' overseas offices. Visa and American Express credit cards are accepted by businesses in many of Latin America's largest cities.

Visas and Passports

Unlike many developing countries in Africa and Asia, few Latin American countries require visitors to obtain visas before their arrival. Instead, most Latin American countries issue visas to visitors when they arrive up at the border or the international airport. However, visa requirements can change as often as governments in Latin America, and that can be quite often indeed. Visitors should check the latest information before leaving home.

Passports are required by most Latin American countries. In the United States, passports may be acquired through regional offices and local post offices. They take about six weeks to be issued.

Responsible Travel

To travel responsibly requires that you realize that the actions you take during your stay in Latin America will continue to affect the lives of the locals and their environment long after you have gone. During your journey, it will be up to you to decide how best to spend your money, how best to protect and preserve the backcountry environment and, if you choose, how best to help the people among whom you'll be traveling.

You can help the local economy by spending as much money as possible at the local level—by staying in local, family-run guest houses, eating at locally owned restaurants and hiring local services where possible. It is just as important to pay close-to-market prices for local goods and services as it is to buy them in the first place. Paying more than market value will only cause local merchants to refuse to sell their goods or services to other locals, choosing to wait for wealthy visitors instead.

Traveling responsibly in the backcountry requires following the principles of minimum-impact camping. Visitors should attempt to leave the areas they visit cleaner than they found them, and should use up as few natural resources as possible. Litter is an obvious no-no. Campfires waste Latin America's diminishing wood resources and should be avoided.

Vaccinations

Depending on where you'll be going in Latin America, vaccines to help your body fend off yellow fever, typhoid and hepatitis may be recommended, as may pills to help prevent malaria. Check with a doctor familiar with the needs of international travelers. Note that many large city hospitals have international clinics serving the growing number of Westerners traveling to the developing world.

Water

The greatest threat to your health in Latin America is impure water. Avoid ingesting all water, tap water or otherwise, unless you know it to be pure. Don't be shy. If the silverware in a restaurant is damp, wipe it dry. And don't eat the fresh salad that has been served to you with dinner. Never eat uncooked foods unless you prepare them yourself using pure water, or unless you peel the food yourself in the case of fruits. Don't brush your teeth with impure water, and don't drink beverages served with ice. Purify all water you ingest. Three methods of water purification exist. Water boiled for ten minutes is considered safe, but that option is generally considered unreasonable because it is fuel-intensive. A tincture of iodine added to water in the form of drops or tablets will kill most any organism lurking there. A water filter is a third option. Water-purification filters range in price from $40 to more than $200. Most outdoor equipment stores carry several types.

Prevention and First-Aid

Visitors to the backcountry of Latin America must know basic prevention and first-aid techniques, since they are often far from professional health-care facilities. They must know how to guard against and/or treat maladies like athlete's foot, blisters, sunburn, hypothermia, frostbite, dehydration, sunstroke, cuts, sprains, colds, flu, diarrhea, constipation, and insect and animal bites.

You may wish to carry some of the following items in your medical kit. (The following list is general in scope. Seek the advice of a physician experienced in international travel to determine exactly which items will be best for your medical kit, how much of each you should carry, and correct dosages.)

Athlete's foot ointment
Blister pads
Sunscreen
Sunscreen lip balm
Petroleum jelly
Skin lotion
Medications for personal skin-related problems like rashes,
    hemorrhoids and cold sores
Insect repellent
Antimalarial medication (if needed)
Topical antibiotic ointment
Bandaids
Adhesive tape and gauze
Antihistamine
Aspirin
Pepto-Bismol tablets
Antibiotics
Antiparasitic drug

What to Bring

The items you take to Latin America can make or break your trip. The most important advice—offered by every guidebook—is to travel as light as possible. Jettison everything but the barest essentials before leaving home. Practice packing several days before you leave. Consider each item as you put it in your backpack or duffel bag. Can you make the item smaller? Lighter? Can you get by without it? Take it only if it's something you absolutely can't do without.

In addition to the suggested medical kit above, the following list should serve as a starting point as you begin gathering gear for your journey.

Suggested List for Group Members

Backpack or duffel bag
Day pack
Water filter (if desired)
Pad, self-inflating
Clothing
Footwear
Scarf/bandanna
Visor or brimmed hat
Sunglasses/neck strap
Alarm watch
Camera/lens
Film
Flashlight
Candle
Water bottle
Food
Knife
Games/playing cards
Travel guidebooks
Language book or dictionary
Reading material
Maps
Laundry detergent
Earplugs
Padlock

Additional Items if Traveling Without Group Support

Sleeping bag
Tent
Stove
Fuel container(s)
Cook kit, including:
  Lighter
  Pot
  Lid / frying pan
  Scrubber
  Mug
  Eating utensils

Passport Holder/Money Belt

Passport
Vaccination card
Credit card
Personal checks
Traveler's checks
Currency - local
Currency - stable
Airline ticket
Paper, pen

Toiletry Kit

Comb
Deodorant
Toilet paper
Toothbrush
Toothpaste
Dental floss
Soap
Shampoo
Towel
Feminine napkins
Tampons
Razor

Emergency Kit

Patch kit for self-inflating pad
Rope
Lighter or matches in waterproof container
Duct tape
Stove repair kit
Sewing kit
Plastic bags
Ziploc-style storage bags
Camera battery
Flashlight batteries, bulb
Iodine

Writing Kit (for lengthy trips)

Note pad
Pens
Address book
Envelopes, stamps
Postcards, aerograms

Descriptions of Listed Items

Address book - For writing all those postcards to folks back home. Leave a copy of the book at home in case you lose yours.

Airline ticket - Best to keep it with you in your passport holder. Most are refundable, but getting a refund in Latin America can be a real chore.

Alarm watch - Crucial for all those buses, trains and planes you'll hurry up and wait around for. Preferable to a heavier, bulkier travel alarm clock.

Backpack or duffel bag - If your gear will be carried by pack animal, bring it in a sturdy duffel bag. Otherwise, an internal-frame backpack is much easier to travel with than is an external-frame pack.

Camera/lens - A pocket 35-mm camera is a good choice, as is a larger, heavier 35-mm SLR camera (preferably with a zoom lens), which produces higher-quality pictures than does a pocket 35-mm camera.

Camera battery - Most of today's cameras require tiny batteries. These batteries are impossible to find in most of Latin America. Find out what your camera needs, and carry an extra (or two, if that's what your camera requires), even if the ones in your camera are brand new.

Candle - For when the moon alone won't do, and the nearest electric line is far away. Candle lanterns are nice, but a candle alone should suffice, since ounces are vital.

Clothing - Decisions concerning what clothing to take to Latin America depend on versatility and weight. The best way to keep clothing weight down is to choose pieces that can be used for several functions. For example, button-up wool shirts are decent for city wear, and they make a nice light-sweater layer when hiking and camping. When planning a cold-weather wardrobe for visits to Latin America's high mountains or to southern Chile or Argentina, be sure to use the principles of layering for warmth. For warm weather, stick with comfortable, loose-fitting clothes. Cotton is the most comfortable fabric to wear in heat, but cotton-poly blends are more wrinkle-free for city wear. For women, slacks are generally acceptable attire, but long skirts earn the locals' appreciation and respect, especially in the backcountry.

For trips in all conditions, the following clothing should be adequate:
3 pairs of underwear
1 bra (women)
1 pair lightweight cotton-poly pants
1 pair cotton-poly drawstring shorts (men)
1 swimsuit (women)
1 calf-length or longer cotton-poly skirt (women)
3 button-up cotton-poly shirts or blouses (at least one with long sleeves)
1 button-up wool shirt
1 outer-shell rain/wind jacket

For trips to warm locales, also bring:
3 pairs of cotton-poly socks

For cold weather, add:
3 pairs of polypropylene sock liners
2 pairs of wool socks
1 synthetic long-underwear shirt
1 pair synthetic long-underwear bottoms
1 pair rain/wind pants
1 heavy sweater or pile jacket

1 down or synthetic vest or jacket
1 pair polypropylene glove liners
1 pair wool mittens
1 pair waterproof overmitts
1 balaclava

Comb - A brush is heavier and bulkier.

Cook kit - If you'll be cooking on your trip, an aluminum cook kit is essential. Stainless steel kits are heavier, although they're sturdier than aluminum kits.

Credit card - Even if you're planning to do all your spending with traveler's checks, a credit card provides a good backup.

Currency - local - Be sure you have plenty before you head for the hills, since places to change traveler's checks into local cash will be rare once you leave the big cities.

Currency - stable - Keep anywhere from one hundred to several hundred dollars of cash with you at all times for emergencies. U.S. dollars are by far the most widely accepted foreign currency in all Latin America.

Day pack - For day hikes and around-town jaunts. A fanny pack works well because it may be worn in front in Latin America's many thief-ridden cities.

Dental floss - Hard to find in most Latin American countries.

Deodorant - It goes a long way toward restoring spirits at the end of a long, sweaty day when no clean-up facilities are available. Bring just a little in a small container.

Duct tape - The bind-all, fix-all tape of choice for the traveling crowd. Wrap a few feet around a pencil to save space (then you'll also have an emergency writing implement).

Earplugs - The inexpensive variety of foam-rubber plugs snipped in half to be less conspicuous are essential to battle the many loud noises in Latin America.

Eating utensils - The best eating utensils, made of unbreakable nylon, are available in outdoor equipment stores.

Envelopes/stamps - If you're a letter writer, keep a few of each handy.

Feminine napkins - Many women find that wearing these every day overseas makes washing their underwear an easy task. The light-day variety isn't too bulky.

Film - Film speed and type—slide or print—is a personal choice. Bring plenty; film available in Latin America is often out of date or stored incorrectly.

Flashlight - Should be small, light and reliable.

Flashlight batteries, bulb - Take a spare set.

Food - All you'll need for camping and backpacking is available in Latin America's cities and towns. Because of the vagaries of travel in Latin America, always keep some snack food handy.

Footwear - On any trip good walking boots or shoes are a necessity. Any of today's wide range of lightweight hiking boots will work well for most hikers. A pair of sturdy, waterproof, velcro-strap sport sandals makes a versatile second pair of shoes. The sandals may be used in unclean showers, on river trips, and for river and stream crossings. They also make good camp shoes since, unlike thongs, they may be worn over socks.

Fuel container(s) - Since it is illegal to transport flammable liquids on an airplane flight, you'll be dependent on the fuels you can find in Latin America (see stove description). Sigg and MSR metal fuel bottles work well.

Games/playing cards - A small magnetic backgammon board, magnetic chess game or deck of cards can help you survive a lengthy bus ride or a long wait for a washed out road to be repaired.

Iodine - Available in tablet or crystal form. Needed as a backup to your water filter or as your primary water purifier.

Knife - You'll use a multi-purpose knife continuously on your trip.

Language book or dictionary - No matter how little of the local language you use, if you use any at all you'll be treated with respect.

Laundry detergent - Unless you're part of a group trip whose workers handle laundry, you'll be diving elbow-deep into water every few days to wash the few clothes you'll be carrying—unless you hire someone to do it. Either way, you'll need to carry some detergent.

Lid/frying pan - To conserve fuel while heating food and liquids, it is important to have a snug-fitting pot lid. The lid will also work as a frying pan and an extra plate.

Lighter - A cheap disposable works great. You'll use it to light your stove or candle, and to burn your toilet paper and other paper trash along the trail.

Lighter or matches in waterproof container - As a backup to your main lighter.

Maps - Generally, stores in the large city or town closest to the backcountry area you'll be visiting will carry maps of the area. Any available maps will make a good addition to the small maps that will be included in your guidebook.

Mug - The bigger the better. I use a plastic, sixteen-ounce measuring cup. It's big enough for soup, oatmeal or stew, but small enough for a cup of coffee.

Note pad - For journal and letter writing.

Pad, self-inflating - Self-inflating sleeping pads aren't cheap, but a single night on one will convince you they're worth the price. A three-quarter-length pad should be adequate unless you'll be sleeping on snow. Fold your pad in half lengthwise before rolling it up—it'll be a lot easier to store in your pack.

Padlock - Locking the zipper on your pack or duffel bag with a small padlock will deter thieves. Some hotels require you to supply your own room lock.

Paper/pen - Good to keep with you in your passport holder for noting ideas you may want to include in your journal or in letters later, and for jotting down information like bus schedules and costs of items you're thinking of buying.

Passport - Keep it on your person under your clothes at all times. Nothing is more valuable to thieves than your passport. Replacing a lost or stolen passport can be a real hassle.

Patch kit for self-inflating pad - Just in case.

Pens - Widely available in Latin America. Just bring a couple.

Personal checks - You'll need a few if you'll be using an American Express card to buy traveler's checks from the company's Latin American offices.

Plastic bags - Rather than a bulky rain cover for your whole backpack, use plastic bags for keeping your gear both organized and dry within your pack.

Postcards, aerograms - Postcards available in Latin America are not generally of high quality, but the scenes they depict are more than clear enough to leave the folks back home filled with envy, which is the main purpose of postcards anyway. Aerograms are simply unfolded envelopes already printed with the amount of postage needed to be delivered anywhere in the world. You write on the inside of the envelope, fold it up and drop it in a mailbox. In most countries, an aerogram is significantly cheaper to send than a traditional letter in an envelope. They're available at post offices and in some stores.

Pot - Make sure it's big enough.

Razor - Disposables are the easiest. Rather than carrying shaving cream, you may choose to save weight by getting along with soap.

Reading material - Books in English are available to a limited extent in Latin American cities and tourist towns. It's also easy to trade books with other visitors.

Rope - Twenty-five to fifty feet of nylon cord is handy as a clothesline and for many other purposes.

Scarf/bandanna - Another item with many uses. It will work as a headband, a hair cover, or a neck cover in bright sunlight. It can also brighten your evening wardrobe, act as a face mask on a dusty truck ride, and be a filter for filling your fuel container.

Scrubber - A plastic pot scrubber eases cleanup.

Sewing kit - Include one or two heavy-duty needles and carpet thread or fishing line for rips and delaminations in your pack and other gear.

Shampoo - Be sure your container doesn't leak.

Sleeping bag - Whether to carry a down-fill or synthetic-fill bag is a personal choice. Down bags are lighter and more compact than synthetic bags, but a damp down bag won't keep you warm while a synthetic bag will.

Soap - Bar soap is available everywhere.

Stove - Automobile gasoline is the cook fuel of choice in much of Latin America, with kerosene a distant second. The stove you take should be able to handle both. Several multi-fuel stoves are on the market.

Stove repair kit - If you'll be doing much of your own cooking, you'll need to maintain and possibly repair your stove. Many stove manufacturers offer kits that enable you to do both.

Sunglasses/neck strap - Be sure they screen out ultraviolet rays, which cause eye damage and headaches.

Tampons - Available only in Latin America's big cities, where they are expensive and selection is limited. Bring your own.

Tent - There are many options to be considered when selecting a tent. The staff at your favorite outdoor equipment store can help you make your selection.

Toilet paper - Always keep plenty on hand.

Toothbrush - A plastic 35-mm film container with a hole in the lid makes a compact case for the head of your toothbrush.

Toothpaste - Widely available. Start with a small travel tube.

Towel - A hand towel should be adequate. It is small and light and dries quickly.

Travel guidebooks - Use this book as a starting point. Also, ask the advice of anyone you know who has been where you're going.

Traveler's checks - American Express traveler's checks are the most widely used and recognized.

Vaccination card - Keep a record of all your vaccinations in your passport holder at all times. You may have to show it when entering a country. Leave a photocopy at home.

Visor or brimmed hat - To fend off the equatorial sun.

Water bottle - A one-liter bottle is probably enough. Bring a sturdy Lexan or Nalgene bottle from home; leakproof plastic bottles are few and far between in Latin America.

Water filter - Useful for lengthy trips. For trips of two to three weeks, iodine is probably adequate.

Ziploc-style storage bags - These are impossible to find in Latin America, but are great to have along. Bring several. You'll use them over and over.

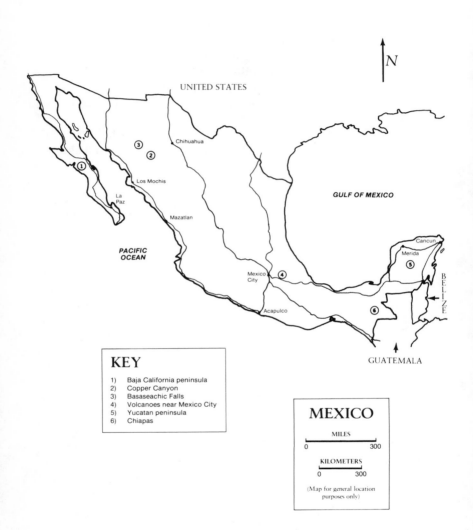

N

UNITED STATES

Chihuahua

③
②

Los Mochis

La
Paz

Mazatlan

PACIFIC
OCEAN

①

GULF OF MEXICO

Cancun

Merida

⑤

B
E
L
I
Z
E

Mexico
City

④

Acapulco

⑥

GUATEMALA

KEY

1) Baja California peninsula
2) Copper Canyon
3) Basaseachic Falls
4) Volcanoes near Mexico City
5) Yucatan peninsula
6) Chiapas

MEXICO

MILES

0   300

KILOMETERS

0   300

(Map for general location
purposes only)

Chapter 5

Mexico

Overview

Realtors often describe the three most important considerations when shopping for a new home as location, location and location.

For those constrained by money, time, or both, location also plays an important role in determining where to vacation. Mexico's location directly south of the United States makes it an understandably popular destination for North American visitors, from tourists enjoying the high life in first-class hotels on the Pacific coast and Yucatan peninsula to budget travelers slinging their hammocks from the walls of hostels in quiet seaside villages.

Between those two extremes, travelers willing to forsake a few creature comforts in return for getting off Mexico's well-worn tourist paths are discovering a variety of adventurous pursuits in North America's southernmost country. From mountain climbing to jungle trekking, and from scuba diving to sea kayaking, Mexico has something for every adventurous traveler's taste.

Inexpensive tourist flights enable visitors to reach tourist centers at minimal cost. Those looking to get away from the tourist hordes have simply to head straight out of town from the airport via local bus or rental car. Visits to the Yucatan and to southern Mexico are perhaps best done this way to avoid the time and discomfort involved in long train, bus or car journeys south from the United States.

Northern Mexico can be visited by bus, train or private car. Trips between points in the United States and Mexican cities as far south as the capital, Mexico City, may be made via Greyhound-Trailways Bus Lines. Train connections must be made right after crossing the border into Mexico, but reservations on the Mexican connections may be made in advance. The two most popular train connection points for visitors from the north are Juarez, across the border from El Paso, Texas, and Nogales, across the border from Nogales, Arizona.

Railroad lines in northern Mexico include the world-renowned southwest-northeast run between Los Mochis and Chihuahua. The route traverses the heart of the Sierra Madre, the mountains that form the backbone of Mexico. It is undoubtedly one of the most beautiful train rides in the world, with 96 tunnels, 36 bridges—the highest a dizzying 335 feet (102 meters) above the ground—and a stop at the edge of *Barranca del Cobre,* or Copper Canyon, actually a system of several deep river gorges so immense it could hold five Grand Canyons.

Special insurance is available—and necessary—for any auto trip in Mexico. Night driving should be avoided. Bring spare parts, particularly air and fuel filters, and budget for at least one major repair bill.

I once visited the Pacific coast of Mexico with my family in a 1968 Pontiac. The Pontiac proved ideal for exploring Mexico. Its sturdy construction stood up to the pounding of Mexico's potholed highways, its powerful eight-cylinder engine kept going no matter how watered down the fuel we fed it. Most important, the trip was worry-free because we were traveling in a car well over fifteen years old: had the Pontiac failed catastrophically, we would simply have bid it a fond adieu and headed home via public transport.

Mexican roads are often in poor condition. Still, they are open to those in their own cars or on bicycles. Buses ranging from plush to ramshackle ply the highways, while trains hold to their comfortably late Latin time schedules. Where roads and railroad tracks end, centuries-old footpaths wind their way to backcountry villages, farms and ranches. Many of these paths are used by descendants of the Indians who were the sole inhabitants of Mexico until the arrival of the Spanish conquistadors in the early 1500s. In the south, the paths wind through thick jungle vegetation buzzing with insects and dripping with moisture. In the north, they climb cactus-choked arroyos and cross immense forested escarpments in the Sierra Madre. Wherever they lead in Mexico, trails offer tremendous opportunities for backpackers who wish to combine wilderness travel with cultural experience. Indeed, many of the Indians visitors meet along the trails continue to speak only the tribal languages of their ancestors rather than Spanish, the primary language of modern Mexico.

Recorded civilization has been traced back to almost 3000 B.C. in Mexico, making it one of the cradles of modern man. The Toltec civilization thrived in central and southern Mexico from several centuries B.C. until nearly a thousand years after Christ's death. The Toltecs are known for the elaborate calendar they developed, and for their construction of the impressive pyramids of Teotihuacan, the ruins of which may be seen near Mexico City.

The Mayan civilization, centered in present-day Guatemala, stretched into southern Mexico and left behind the Palenque ruins in the state of Chiapas, Chichen Itza and surrounding ruins on the Yucatan peninsula, and others along the Mexico-Guatemala border.

The highly advanced Aztec civilization controlled much of modern Mexico at the time of the arrival of the conquistadors. The Aztecs fell to the Spanish conquistadors and their Indian allies after several years of bitter battles. The Spaniards placed a veneer of Catholicism over the Aztec religion, which had revered many gods. The mixed religion that resulted is practiced in much of rural Mexico to this day.

More intermarriage took place in Mexico between Indians and Spaniards than in other parts of Latin America. As a result, well over half of Mexico's population of some 80 million people is *mestizo*, or mixed blood. Three in ten Mexicans are full-blooded Indians. Many of Mexico's Indian tribes remain semi-autonomous, living on the fringes of modern civilization in rural areas throughout the country.

The gap between the haves and have-nots is wide in Mexico. Among the have-nots, unemployment is estimated to be close to 50 percent. It is the extreme poverty faced by many Mexicans that has caused ever-increasing numbers to forsake their homeland and cross the border into the United States illegally, in search of better lives.

Geography

Mexico serves as a bridge between the broad United States to the north and the narrow Central American isthmus in the south. In addition to its 1,950-mile (3,150-kilometer) border with the United States, Mexico borders on Belize and Guatemala in the south. Mexico is bordered by the Pacific Ocean on the west and the Gulf of Mexico on the east. With an area of more than 760,000 square miles (2 million square kilometers), Mexico is roughly one-quarter the combined size of the United States' lower 48 states.

Mexico is primarily a land of coastlines and mountains. Two peninsulas add distinctive character to the country, Baja California in the northwest and the Yucatan peninsula in the southeast. The two peninsulas are very different. Baja is narrow and rugged, marked by a spine of sharp, dry mountains rising as high as 10,000 feet (3,000 meters). The Yucatan is broad and wet. In its flat, jungled interior are numerous Mayan ruins, including those of the sacred Mayan city of Chichen Itza.

The primary mountains of Mexico are those of the Sierra Madre, whose three ranges cover much of the country. The Sierra Madre Occidental runs along the Pacific coast of northern Mexico, the Sierra Madre Oriental rises near the Gulf of Mexico, and the Sierra Madre del Sur is in southern Mexico. Northern Mexico is primarily a harsh, barren land of low-lying deserts broken by abrupt ridges of the Sierra Madre. Its allure lies in the starkness of its deserts, the beauty of its high mountain forests and the serenity of the thousands of miles of mostly undeveloped beaches that line its coasts. In the tropical, fertile south, the crest of the Sierra Madre del Sur follows the Pacific coastline's eastward bend as Mexico narrows toward the Central American isthmus.

Several volcanoes near Mexico City rise above the perpetual snow line. The easternmost of the volcanoes, Orizaba, tops out at 18,700 feet (5,700 meters), the highest point in Mexico.

Climate

Much of Mexico lies south of the Tropic of Cancer and is thus part of the tropics. As a result of this proximity to the equator, Mexico's generally warm temperatures don't vary a great deal from season to season. Only in the north are temperatures appreciably cooler in winter than in summer. Most rain in the north falls during the blazing summers. The combination of oppressive heat and sudden rainstorms makes summer the worst time to visit. Instead, northern Mexico is ideal in the spring and fall.

Only in the extreme south does much rain fall in Mexico. In Chiapas, which borders Guatemala, the annual rainfall often exceeds 150 inches (380 centimeters). The Yucatan, by comparison, averages 60 inches (150 centimeters) of rain each year. Southern Mexico is hot and humid year round. The rainy season runs from May to October, but rain can fall anytime. The best months to visit southern Mexico are from November to March, when rain is least likely and temperatures are coolest.

Adventure-Travel Possibilities

The **Baja California peninsula (1)** has become increasingly popular with travelers over the last few years. As a result, solitude is an increasingly scarce commodity, even though the peninsula stretches south from the state of California for nearly 1,000 miles (1,600 kilometers). Still, Baja offers visitors a wide variety of adventurous possibilities and numerous secluded beaches. A paved highway runs the length of Baja.

Pastimes on the Baja include beach camping, windsurfing, diving, fishing, sailing, sea kayaking, backpacking, horse packing, bicycle touring and whale watching. Many tours to Baja sponsored by U.S.-based companies enable participants to sample any of these activities.

Gray whales migrate from the frigid Bering Sea to Scammon's Lagoon and other bays on the Pacific coast of Baja every year between late January and early March to bear their young in warm southern waters. The whales of Scammon's Lagoon, about halfway down the peninsula, may be viewed from coastal hills near the town of Guerrero Negro or from the decks of the few tour boats allowed on the lagoon during the breeding season. Scammon's Lagoon has been designated a marine national park by the Mexican government.

Other protected areas of Baja follow.

* Tiny Constitution of 1857 National Park in far northern Baja California near San Diego and Tijuana contains Hanson Lake with its variety of bird life. Camping is available in the park.

* Hikers and backpackers enjoy Sierra de San Pedro Martir National Park. The park contains 10,154-foot (3,095-meter) Picacho del Diablo, the highest point on the peninsula. The peak is located in the north-central part of Baja, and is often dusted with snow in winter. Pleasant hiking trails wind through the park. Climbing the rugged Picacho del Diablo is only for the experienced.

* Midriff Islands Wildlife Sanctuary encompasses several remote desert islands off the east coast of the Baja. The islands are popular with sea kayakers and sailors looking to explore out-of-the-way locales. The flora and fauna of these central Baja islands is so diverse—with many species unique to particular islands—that the islands are known as the Galapagos of the north.

Barranca del Cobre, or **Copper Canyon (2),** is located in the heart of the Sierra Madre Occidental in north-central Mexico. It is truly one of the natural wonders of the world. My first visit to the canyon was via the Los Mochis-to-Chihuahua train. I wasn't prepared money-, time- or equipment-wise to stay, yet the view of the canyon was so spectacular it was all I could do to climb back aboard the train after its 20-minute gawk-stop at the canyon rim.

Copper Canyon is a series of steep gorges created by several rivers carving through the area's high mountains, which reach 9,000 feet (2,750 meters) at some points and are snow-covered in winter. In addition to the train, the region may be reached by road. Several hotels on the canyon's rim cater to visitors. Some offer hiking and horse-packing tours of the canyon's depths. Hiking is also popular in the mountain areas above the canyon. The entire area is populated by the proud, reclusive Tarahumara Indians, who continue to follow their traditional ways despite the conquistadors, miners, lumbermen and tourists who have passed through their homeland over the centuries.

Backpacker magazine calls the entire Copper Canyon "a backpacker's paradise." Indeed it is. The various gorges in the region range in elevation from 8,000 feet (2,450 meters) at the rim to close to 1,000 feet (300 meters) at the bottom. The climate varies just as widely. Temperatures on the canyon rim often fall below freezing at night, while the climate at the bottom of the gorges is subtropical.

Footpaths used for centuries by the Tarahumara, known for their tremendous running ability, wind up and down the gorges of Copper Canyon. Independent backpackers may set out to explore the gorges from any of a number of small towns perched on the canyon rim or hidden deep in the river bottoms at the ends of rugged dirt roads. These include Divisadero, reached only by train; Creel, reached by train and paved road; and the tiny, tropical town of Batopilas, at the end of a rugged dirt road deep in a side gorge of the Urique River. Note that unlike in other parts of northern Mexico, hikes in the depths of Copper Canyon are best undertaken in the middle of winter when temperatures are coolest.

Northwest of Copper Canyon near the town of Tomachic is 1,000-foot (300-meter) **Basaseachic Falls (3),** highest in Mexico. Trails lead from the nearest road to the top and bottom of the falls. Other trails lead deep into the little-explored region surrounding the falls.

Three high volcanoes near Mexico City (4)—also the three highest points in Mexico—are particularly popular with climbers. In addition to 18,700-foot (5,700-meter) Orizaba, they include 17,887-foot (5,452-meter) Popocatepetl, known as Popo, and 17,343-foot (5,286-meter) Ixtaccihuatl, commonly called Ixta.

The volcanoes are excellent climbs for those who want to give snow climbing at altitude a try. Crampons, ice axes and ropes are necessary. Huts on the mountains make tents unnecessary, although the huts can be crowded on weekends and during the best climbing months, December and January.

There are those who believe the development of the city of Cancun and the nearby island of Cozumel as resort areas has destroyed the relaxed, friendly milieu that once greeted all visitors to the remote **Yucatan peninsula (5)** in southeastern Mexico. Those people have a point. On the other hand, the Yucatan's resorts are adding desperately needed hard currency to the Mexican economy while assuring that the Yucatan will remain little industrialized and continue to draw large numbers of tourists to what is now a natural wonderland.

In addition, direct tourist flights at low fares now make the Yucatan easily accessible to travelers planning to visit other, less developed parts of the peninsula. Before the development of Cancun and Cozumel as destination resorts, travelers to the Yucatan faced expensive flights to Merida, the largest city on the peninsula, or long train and bus rides from Mexico City.

Merida may still be reached by train or long-distance bus. From there, rental cars are available, or local buses travel to virtually every town on the peninsula. Rental cars and Jeeps are also available in Cancun. The road system on the Yucatan has been steadily upgraded over the last few years. Today, paved roads stretch throughout the peninsula.

Many small seaside villages offer excellent alternatives to Cancun and Cozumel. Tulum, south of Cancun along the coast, is popular with the budget crowd. Isla Mujeres, a coastal island near Cancun, is fast developing as a destination resort area. For now, however, the island is a relaxed destination boasting good snorkeling and diving. Visitors may choose from a variety of mid-priced hotels on the island.

The most impressive (and most popular) ruin on the Yucatan is Chichen Itza, a sacred city of both Mayan and Toltec architecture. The ruins, spread over several square miles, include numerous temples, a huge pyramid, tombs, intricately carved columns, and an observatory. There are hotels in the area if one day at the site isn't enough.

Uxmal, an hour's drive south of Merida, is the second most popular ruin on the Yucatan. The city of Uxmal was rebuilt five times over the course of its habitation; each reconstruction was more elaborate than the last. Uxmal is actually the largest of several ancient Mayan ruins in the area, and is the most ornate ruin yet found on the peninsula. All the ruins may be visited over the course of one or several days using nearby Merida as a base.

Perhaps the most fascinating region in Mexico is the state of **Chiapas (6)** in the extreme south. In Chiapas are Palenque, one of the most impressive ruins in Mexico, and intriguing backcountry areas covered by dense rainforest and populated by Indians.

Palenque may be reached by road or train from Mexico City and Merida. The ancient jungle city is on the list of must-see Mayan ruins, along with Chichen Itza, Tikal in Guatemala and Copan in Honduras. Palenque features steep pyramid temples that loom above the jungle canopy, numerous plazas and tombs, and a four-story tower once part of the city's immense palace complex.

Nearby is Agua Azul, a river of bright blue water cascading over limestone formations. Behind the formation outcroppings are pools ideal for swimming. Camping beside the river is popular.

A good base for exploring the Chiapas backcountry is the popular tourist town of San Cristobal de las Casas, 150 miles (240 kilometers) southwest of Palenque. This Indian town is located high in the mountains at nearly 7,000 feet (2,150 meters). The altitude makes San Cristobal a pleasant retreat from the oppressive heat of Mexico's southern lowlands. Day hikes in the area lead to remote villages.

The beaches of Mexico are a world unto themselves. Many visitors to the country don't bother with the interior at all, choosing instead to spend every minute on the coast—for good reason. Mexico's seas and shores offer visitors a variety of activities, ranging from lying on warm sand beside lapping waves to maneuvering an ocean-equipped catamaran through rolling breakers against a stiff headwind.

The best areas for snorkeling and diving are found off the Yucatan peninsula, where coral reefs provide shelter for tropical fish and other sea creatures. Diving is also popular off southern Baja. The peninsula is also a popular destination for surfers and windsurfers. Sea kayakers enjoy the waters of the protected Gulf of California between Baja and the Mexican mainland. Sailors of everything from small catamarans to luxurious yachts take advantage of the Pacific coast's steady breezes to explore the length of Mexico's west coast.

The best beach camping in Mexico is found on Baja, south of Cancun on the Yucatan's Gulf coast, and on the many remote stretches of beach between the resort cities of Mazatlan, Puerto Vallarta and Acapulco on Mexico's west coast.

Information Sources

The Bible of budget travelers to Mexico is *Mexico: A Travel Survival Kit* (Lonely Planet Publications). Since the book encourages off-the-beaten-path exploration of the country—and details many such possibilities—its purchase is recommended for any adventure travelers planning to explore a great deal of Mexico.

If you'll be visiting only a certain part of Mexico, you'll likely be better off buying one or more of the many guides available that detail specific areas of the country.

For Baja California, Wilderness Press' *The Baja Adventure Book* describes every conceivable adventurous pastime visitors might consider during a trip to the peninsula, and offers advice on the best places to engage in each. The book's exhaustive hand-drawn maps are particularly noteworthy.

In the usual Lonely Planet Publications mold, *Baja California: A Travel Survival Kit* is a good, down-to-earth guide for independent visitors to the peninsula. The book's author, Scott Wayne, does an admirable job of listing affordable accommodations on the peninsula, where budget hostels are being replaced by more expensive hotels as Baja's popularity increases. Wayne also provides a detailed list of the many tour operators offering trips to Baja.

The self-published book *National Parks of Northwest Mexico* (Sunracer Publications, P.O. Box 40092, Tucson, AZ 85187) is commendable both for its coverage of little-explored parks in northern Mexico and for the author's commitment to encouraging the preservation and protection of the flora, fauna and native Indians of northwestern Mexico. In this bilingual book, author Richard Fisher provides information on canyoneering techniques, tales drawn from many visits to northwest Mexico, and general information on visiting the national parks of the region.

Chicki Mallan's *Guide to the Yucatan Peninsula* (Moon Publications) provides a detailed look at everything there is to see and do in the three states composing Mexico's share of the Yucatan *and* in the country's two southernmost states, Tabasco and Chiapas.

Mallan's emphasis is on avoiding resort areas and instead finding southern Mexico's hidden wonders.

Hidden Mexico: Adventurer's Guide to the Beaches and Coasts (Ulysses Press) delivers what its title promises: information on where to find the remaining secluded beaches and coastlines of Mexico and what to do once you're there. Author Rebecca Bruns spent ten months exploring Mexico's coasts in a 1978 Toyota, and so offers good first-hand advice to anyone considering travel by car in Mexico.

Backpacking in Mexico and Central America (Bradt Publications) describes hiking and mountain-climbing opportunities in three areas of Mexico: Copper Canyon, the central volcanoes and Chiapas.

For those who will be climbing any of the high volcanoes of central Mexico, *Mexico's Volcanoes: A Climbing Guide* (The Mountaineers) is a must. The book describes climbing routes on six central Mexico volcanoes, including Orizaba, Popo and Ixta.

Carl Franz' *The People's Guide to Mexico* (John Muir Publications) offers plenty of how-to advice, but not much where-to. Franz is a great storyteller. His uproarious descriptions of the scrapes he has survived during his travels in Mexico make terrific reading.

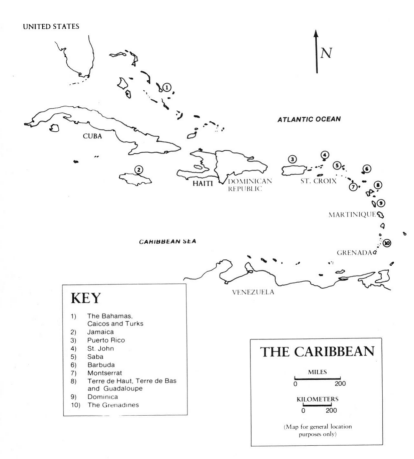

UNITED STATES

N

ATLANTIC OCEAN

CUBA

HAITI DOMINICAN
REPUBLIC

ST. CROIX

MARTINIQUE

CARIBBEAN SEA

GRENADA

VENEZUELA

KEY

1) The Bahamas,
   Caicos and Turks
2) Jamaica
3) Puerto Rico
4) St. John
5) Saba
6) Barbuda
7) Montserrat
8) Terre de Haut, Terre de Bas
   and Guadaloupe
9) Dominica
10) The Grenadines

THE CARIBBEAN

MILES
0   200

KILOMETERS
0   200

(Map for general location
purposes only)

Chapter 6

The Caribbean

Overview

The islands of the Caribbean Sea, known collectively as the West Indies, don't seem to lend themselves to adventure travel. Instead, the first activity that comes to mind is lying on a spectacular but crowded beach or beside a free-form resort pool beneath rustling palm trees. Golf and tennis are about as adventurous as travel gets in the Caribbean, one might think.

Closer examination proves that kind of thinking false. Hundreds of tropical islands dot the Caribbean, and only a few are overrun by high-rise, meticulously manicured resorts. The vast majority are quiet, backwater isles waiting to be explored by independent-minded travelers. Furthermore, even resort-laden islands like Barbados and St. John have hideaway coves and secluded hiking trails for those looking to get away from the glitter for a few hours. On virtually every island in the West Indies there are remote areas that lend themselves to activities like hiking, climbing, sea kayaking, or simply snorkeling and lazing about on secluded beaches.

The West Indies' reputation as a vacation paradise is based on natural features. Coral reefs lie a few feet beneath crystal blue waters. White sand beaches are fringed by palm trees. Verdant rainforests gird soaring volcanic peaks. Plenty of natural areas remain unspoiled, uncrowded and waiting to be explored. None of the islands, however, has the ancient native culture that attracts visitors to other Latin American countries. Instead, each island reflects the cultural heritage of the people who settled there during the colonial days of the 16th, 17th and 18th centuries.

Many of the Indians who once inhabited the West Indies died soon after the arrival of European explorers in the late 1400s and early 1500s. Christopher Columbus and later explorers brought with them diseases with which the natives' immune systems could not cope. Slaves from Africa replaced the natives as laborers for the islands' European colonizers. Today, the islands of the Caribbean are a colorful blend of blacks and Europeans descended from the slaves and colonialists of earlier times.

As a result of its varied colonial past, the Caribbean is one of the few areas in Latin America where Spanish is not uniformly the predominant language. For example, English is the first language of the former British colony of Jamaica, French is the predominant language of neighboring Haiti, formerly a French colony, and Spanish is spoken in the Dominican Republic, which shares the island of Hispaniola with Haiti. In general, however, English and, if necessary, the dedicated use of a Spanish-English or French-English dictionary and phrase book will get you by virtually anywhere in the Caribbean.

Reaching the main islands of the West Indies is simple. Regularly scheduled flights connect North America with all the popular resort islands. Travel to the more remote, quiet and generally smaller islands is a bit more problematic. Often, you'll need to use the nearest resort island as a stopover point from which to reach the remote island you wish to visit, by small plane if a landing strip exists, or by ferry. Small-plane flights in the Caribbean can be expensive. After you arrive at your destination island, however, you'll be spending so much less for food, lodging and entertainment than you would on a resort island that you'll quickly make up for the cost of the additional flight. Further, small-plane flights in the Caribbean are often worth their cost simply for the thrill of flying low over azure seas, coral reefs and tiny, jungled islands.

No matter where you go, travel in the West Indies isn't cheap. Prices of restaurant and store-bought food are equal to or greater than those in North America. Rental-car prices likewise equal or surpass those in North America. And you'll be lucky to find lodging for less than $50 a night.

Geography

The West Indies stretch 2,800 miles (4,500 kilometers) in an arc across the Caribbean. They are bounded by the United States to the northwest, Mexico and Central America to the west, and South America to the south. To the east and northeast, the islands are open to the Atlantic Ocean. Caribbean islands outside this central arc lie near, and are governed by, various Central and South

American countries. In this book, they are covered with those countries.

The largest islands of the West Indies are located at the northwest end of the arc. Cuba's 44,000-square-mile (114,000-square-kilometer) area—about the size of Pennsylvania—makes it the biggest Caribbean island. Haiti and the Dominican Republic share Hispaniola, the next largest of the West Indies. Cuba and Hispaniola do not offer much to the adventure traveler. After Hispaniola in size come Jamaica and Puerto Rico. While these two islands are big in comparison to the rest of the West Indies, the combined area of Jamaica and Puerto Rico does not even equal that of Massachusetts.

The lack of size of the West Indies limits the scope of onshore adventure travel on the islands. The expedition-style tours available in other Latin American countries are simply not possible on any of the island republics of the Caribbean except Jamaica. Instead, visitors may enjoy a variety of adventurous water sports. On land, they must settle for day hikes that generally require no more than a pair of sneakers and a bottle of sunscreen. Only the climbs of a few of the highest peaks of the islands are exceptions. They can be cool, wet and rugged.

Most of the West Indies are steep and mountainous, as a result of their volcanic origin. Unlike rainforests in the rest of Latin America, the rainforests of the West Indies exist only at high altitudes, where warm air rising up the mountainsides mixes with cooler air to produce rain. As a result, hiking in the mountains is often an adventure of hacking through jungle overgrowth and tripping over the meandering, gnarled roots of giant hardwood trees. Conversely, many coastal areas of the West Indies are almost desertlike in their dryness.

Climate

The Caribbean boasts great weather conditions. Because of the stabilizing effects of the northeast trade winds and the Gulf current, temperatures change little from summer to winter or from day to night. Instead, temperatures throughout the islands hold fairly steady in the 80- to 90-degree (30-degree centigrade) range. Only at high altitudes do temperatures drop noticeably.

Rain, too, isn't nearly the problem it is in other parts of Latin America. While the wettest months in the West Indies are from May or June to October, on most islands those months are barely wetter than the winter months. When rain does fall, it generally does so only as a short afternoon shower. In fact, a surprising number of Caribbean islands are arid and face serious water-supply problems.

The jutting peaks of some islands create conditions for daily precipitation. For example, El Yunque, Puerto Rico's concentrated rainforest, receives up to 180 inches (450 centimeters) of rain each year. The same effect makes one side of some islands a verdant, tropical jungle while the other side, perhaps only a few miles away, may receive so little precipitation that cacti barely survive. The lack of heavy precipitation in most of the West Indies means bugs aren't as much of a problem in the Caribbean as elsewhere in Latin America. You'll still want to bring bug repellent along, however, for your forays into the rainforest.

The only negative to all this good news about the climate of the West Indies is the Caribbean's infamous hurricane season. July, August and September are the worst months for hurricanes in the West Indies.

Adventure-Travel Possibilities

The possibilities for adventurous travel in the West Indies are similar from island to island. Generally, the less built-up an island is with resorts and their trappings, the more opportunities there are for you to explore, camp and travel on your own. Notable exceptions do exist, however. Jamaica is large enough to accommodate built-up resort areas and also large tracts of mountainous backcountry excellent for hiking. On other, smaller islands, growth has been concentrated on the coasts, leaving the interiors unspoiled.

As those who sail undoubtedly know, sailboats large enough to sleep several people may be rented on many Caribbean islands. Island-hopping by rented boat—known as bareboating—is popular among those who have both the experience and money to undertake such an adventure. Prices for renting a 30- to 50-foot (10- to 15-meter) sailboat range from $2,000 to $4,000 a week. The most popular islands for bareboating are the U.S. and British Virgin Islands east of Puerto Rico. Rental boats are available on the island of St. Thomas in the U.S. Virgin Islands and on Tortola in the British Virgin Islands.

Rather than bareboating, you may wish to join one of the many sailing-vessel tours that take small groups from one island to another. The trips last a week or two and usually include stays in both quiet coves and bustling ports.

Sea kayaking is another, far less expensive form of water travel growing in popularity on the islands. Since you must bring your own boat from home, inflatable kayaks are most popular. You won't cover as much territory as a rent-a-sloop or a tour vessel, but if you choose the island or islands you visit with care, meandering from deserted cove to deserted cove can be a wonderful adventure.

The West Indies also provide countless prime locations for those hooked on the fast-growing sport of windsurfing. Sailboards are available for rent only in large towns and resorts. For those willing to bring their boards with them, however, the possibilities are endless.

Besides the more unusual pastimes like bareboating, windsurfing and sea kayaking, the most common—and equally enjoyable—outdoor activities on the islands are hiking, snorkeling and diving. The following is a look at some of the best places in the West Indies to undertake those activities.

The Bahamas, Caicos and Turks (1): These small, remote islands, stretching southeastward from Florida, are suitable for day hiking, camping and snorkeling far from crowds and resorts. The islands are known for their cleanliness, and the English-speaking residents (many are descended of British loyalists who left the United States for the islands at the end of the Revolutionary War) are known for their friendliness.

The best islands for adventurous exploration include Long Island, a popular dive center; the small Exumas Islands, from which you can explore the even smaller, uninhabited Lee Stocking Island with its miles of secluded beaches; North Caicos Island, popular with nature lovers and beach lovers alike; and rugged Middle Caicos, whose white-sand beaches are guarded by towering limestone cliffs laced with unexplored, stalactite-filled caves.

Jamaica (2): Jamaica is the only island in the Caribbean that supports overland adventure-travel journeys like those in other parts of Latin America. Although the island is heavily settled, the steep Blue Mountains that form the spine of eastern Jamaica and the remote hills and sinkholes known as the Cockpits in western Jamaica are too rugged for agriculture or ranching. Instead, they remain the realm of the hiker, the backpacker and the river runner. The climb to the top of 7,388-foot (2,252-meter) Blue Peak, the highest of the Blue Mountains, is popular and the trail well maintained.

The beaches of Jamaica—as spectacular as any in the Caribbean—are fairly well developed. Bike touring around the coast and through the interior of the island is popular.

Puerto Rico (3): Long a popular destination for resort-bound sun worshippers, Puerto Rico is slowly building a reputation as a great destination for nature lovers as well. The island is popular with bird watchers. El Yunque rainforest, protected as part of Caribbean National Forest, is the only tropical rainforest in the U.S. National Forest system. Well-maintained hiking trails wind through the forest and several are long enough for overnight backpacking trips.

Just off the east coast of Puerto Rico lies the little-visited island of Culebra, with its deserted beaches and its excellent snorkeling and scuba diving. The island rises only 300 feet (90 meters) above the sea, yet is home to a wide variety of wildlife, including giant lizards, sea turtles and nearly a hundred bird species. The island's mangrove forests provide good hiking possibilities, as does Culebra National Wildlife Refuge, which protects a dry subtropical forest of thorn thickets, palms and cacti.

St. John (4): One of the U.S. Virgin Islands east of Puerto Rico, St. John is often called the most beautiful island in the Caribbean. St. John is by no means remote, but it is popular with nature lovers because about half the island is maintained in its natural state as Virgin Island National Park. Hiking trails wind through the park to beautiful coves and beaches. If money isn't a question, you may choose to stay at the Rockefeller-built Caneel Bay Plantation resort, with its "authentic" jungle vegetation imported from Fiji, for a mere $300 to $600 a night. Otherwise, camping is available at Cinnamon Bay campground in the national park.

Saba (5): Saba is one of the many tiny Leeward Islands southeast of the U.S. and British Virgin Islands. The 5-square-mile (13-square-kilometer) island is a great destination for walkers and hikers. For many years, Saba was considered so rugged it was believed no road could ever be constructed on the island. Instead, long, winding stairways led up and down the steep hills of the island from one side to the other. A serpentine road was eventually constructed that connects one side of the island with the other. Otherwise, the island is open to exploration only on foot. Many of the original stairway trails still exist or have been rebuilt in recent years, including the grueling stairway to the top of Mount Scenery, the highest point on the island at 2,854 feet (870 meters). Although the rocky island has no beaches, snorkeling and diving are superb.

Barbuda (6): Barbuda is the low-lying sister island to Antigua, the island of flashy, new resort fame. Sixty-square-mile (155-square-kilometer) Barbuda tops out at only 143 feet (44 meters) in elevation. Unlike Antigua 25 miles (40 kilometers) away, Barbuda is neither soaring nor verdant, so it will never attract huge resort complexes. Instead, Barbuda's magic lies in its beaches—miles and miles of them, spectacular and deserted. Barbuda's extensive coral reefs, which teem with sea life, have snared many unwary vessels. Those underwater wrecks are especially attractive to divers.

Montserrat (7): This small Leeward island is a wonderland of steep mountains, verdant rainforests, plunging waterfalls and black-sand beaches. Hiking trails wind throughout the island. Montserrat's personable, English-speaking people are building additional trails to attract more nature lovers to the island.

Terre de Haut, Terre de Bas and Guadeloupe (8): Terre de Haut and Terre de Bas are but specks in the Caribbean—but what specks they are. Both are idyllic for walkers, beach lovers, swimmers and snorkelers. There are only a dozen vehicles on Terre de Haut, the more bustling of the two islands. Terre de Haut is connected to neighboring Guadeloupe, 7 miles (11 kilometers) away, by regular hop-scotch flights and small ferries. You may reach Terre de Bas, on the other hand, only by irregular ferry from Guadeloupe or by hiring a fishing boat to take you there from Terre de Haut—provided you speak enough French to explain what you want.

Guadeloupe, the larger, more developed stopover island en route to the two Terres, is popular in its own right for the rugged and not-so-rugged trails that wind through its mountainous national parks.

Dominica (9): Mountainous Dominica is considered by many the lushest, most verdant island of the West Indies. Half of Dominica is rainforest. Fully 80 percent of the island remains in its natural state, and much of the island can be seen only on foot. Extensive hiking trails allow walkers to view Dominica's plant life up close. Beyond those trails, much of the island remains unexplored to this day. A walk on the island, writes Leonard Adkins in

A Walking Guide to the Caribbean, is "as close as one can possibly come to experiencing the Caribbean as it was for centuries before the first settlers arrived."

The Grenadines (10): The 120 Grenadine Islands are spread over a 50-mile (80-kilometer) area north of the Venezuelan coast between St. Vincent and Grenada. Only 11 of the Grenadines are inhabited; virtually every one of the islands is known for its quiet beaches and secluded coves. You may choose to stay at any of several of the Grenadines' tranquil, inhabited islands, like Carriacou, Union or Bequia. Better yet, bring along your camping gear and arrange to have a hired boat drop you off on one of the spectacular uninhabited Grenadines for a few days of playing Robinson Crusoe.

Information Sources

Two excellent books have been published recently for those looking to visit remote, secluded parts of the Caribbean. They are *Undiscovered Islands of the Caribbean*, by Burl Willes (John Muir Publications), and *A Walking Guide to the Caribbean*, by Leonard Adkins (Johnson Publishing Company).

Undiscovered Islands of the Caribbean is a welcome addition to bookstore travel sections otherwise filled with Caribbean guidebooks steering their readers to the mega-resort islands of the West Indies like 13-mile-long (21-kilometer-long) St. Thomas, which plays host to more than a million visitors a year. Willes tells his readers where, how and when to avoid the resorts and find true bliss on the many tranquil, idyllic islands of the Caribbean.

Adkins' walking guide to the Caribbean is excellent as far as it goes. The author covers the islands from the U.S. Virgin Islands southeastward to Martinique. Not covered are the Bahamas, Turks and Caicos, Jamaica, Hispaniola, Puerto Rico and the many islands south of Martinique, including the Grenadines. Two fine guides to traveling off the beaten path in Jamaica are *Guide to Jamaica,* by Harry Pariser (Moon Publications), and the aptly titled *Adventure Guide to Jamaica,* by Steve Cohen (Hunter Publishing, Inc.). Both Pariser and Cohen key on opportunities to explore Jamaica's quieter, more remote areas.

Pariser has also written Moon Publications' *Guide to Puerto Rico and the Virgin Islands,* which is also aimed at helping visitors find the quieter side to these popular resort islands.

In *Latin America on Bicycle* (Passport Press), J.P. Panet includes a chapter chronicling a week-long bike tour of the Dominican Republic.

If you're considering bareboating in the Caribbean, you may wish to track down the December 11, 1988, edition of the *New York Times* at your local library. On page 15 of that issue's travel section is **"The Caribbean Under Sail On One's Own,"** a detailed article on the intricacies and costs of bareboating.

For general, overall information on visiting the Caribbean, try *Fodor's Caribbean and the Bahamas* (Fodor's Travel Guides), or *Frommer's Dollarwise Guide to the Caribbean* (Simon and Schuster, Inc.).

MEXICO

Orange
Walk

Ambergris
Caye

Caye
Caulker

⑥

①

Belize
City

②

GUATEMALA

Belmopan

④

③

Dangriga

Maya Mountains

CARIBBEAN
SEA

⑤

Punta
Gorda

N

BELIZE

MILES

0   25

KILOMETERS

0   25

(Map for general location
purposes only)

KEY

1)   Coral reef and cayes
2)   Turneffe Islands
3)   Mountain Pine Ridge Reserve
4)   San Ignacio —
       Benque Viejo area
5)   San Pedro Colombia — San
       Antonio area
6)   Crooked Tree Wildlife Refuge

Chapter 7

Belize

Overview

Belize may well be the perfect destination for those undertaking their first adventure-travel journey—especially for those doing so independently rather than with an organized group. The small country is wildly exotic, yet it is affordable and easily accessible.

The country offers much for snorkelers and scuba divers. Inland, the country's thickly overgrown backcountry hides deserted Mayan ruins and intriguing mountain paths.

Belize is often described as a slice of Caribbean culture attached to the Central American isthmus. The first modern settlement of Belize was by English traders who brought black slaves from Jamaica in the mid-1600s to log the area's forests. Descendants of those slaves make up the majority of Belize's population today. They speak a colorful, Creole version of English—pleasing to the ear, yet sometimes difficult for visitors to understand. Luckily, the Creoles have no problem speaking a clearer version of their dialect. As a result, English-speaking visitors don't face the language barrier they face in much of Latin America.

Belize City is the largest city in Belize. It is the country's capital in all but name—Belmopan is the official capital. Keep your wits about you in Belize City—thievery is a problem in the city during the day; outright robbery is not uncommon after dark.

To reach Belize, travelers can fly directly to Belize City or travel overland from Guatemala or Mexico. Since the country is just south of the Yucatan peninsula, you may be able to save money by purchasing one of the low-cost excursion fares available from many North American cities to the resort city of Cancun in the

Yucatan. From there, you can travel to Belize overland by bus or rental car. The bus ride from Cancun to Belize City takes about five hours and costs only a few dollars.

By road via Mexico, Belize City is 1,350 miles (2,175 kilometers) from Brownsville, Texas. That distance may be covered by private car or public bus. Train service is available as far south as Merida, Mexico, the capital of Yucatan. Be sure to become familiar with the potential difficulties of auto travel in Mexico (and Belize, for that matter) if you decide to drive your own vehicle.

Belize is slightly smaller than New Hampshire. The country's relatively few citizens—only 160,000 people call Belize home—are scattered sparsely throughout the country. For backcountry enthusiasts, the result is ample territory for hiking. In addition to the Creoles who make up a little more than half of Belize's population, the country includes among its citizens distinct Chinese, northern European, East Indian, Lebanese and Spanish-Indian minorities. There is even a tight-knit group of 3,000 German-speaking Mennonites in the Orange Walk area of northern Belize. They are Belize's premier farmers and poultry producers.

Politically, Belize has been stable since it received its independence from England in 1981. However, British troops have remained since then, because Guatemala has voiced its desire to take over the country.

Belize's economy is based on the export of sugar, fruit, lumber and fish. While the country's standard of living is at the developing-world level, Belizeans are not as desperately poor as citizens of many developing countries. For visitors, travel in Belize is inexpensive compared to the West Indies, but it is not as cheap as in most Latin American nations. Still, your money will go a long way during your visit. American dollars are accepted just about everywhere in the country. They can also be traded for Belizean dollars, which are worthless beyond the country's borders.

Budget hotels charge $5 to $15 a night for a room, while nicer hotel prices range from $25 a night to well over $100. Imported foods are expensive; local produce is just the opposite. A friend who visited Belize a couple of years ago reported buying seven lobsters for $1 from a local fisherman. She and her fellow travelers then cooked them over a fire on the beach for the lobster feast of a lifetime.

Travel within Belize is affordable, too. Even flying is cheap, because flights are short in the tiny country. The fare from Belize City's municipal airport to Ambergris Caye (pronounced "key") off the coast is only about $30 each way. Flights are also available to other cities on the mainland. Since Belize is so small, you may wonder why you should consider flying from one mainland city to another. One bus ride will provide your answer: Belizean roads, like many in Latin America, are extremely rough. Dirt roads may be impassable for days or even weeks during the rainy season. The pavement of some roads is so worn that traffic is confined to the shoulders. In addition, mangrove swamps cover much of the Belizean coast. Although the country's largest towns are on the coast, you must travel far inland to avoid the swamps, then north or south before returning to the coast at your chosen destination.

Despite these problems, as the tourism industry grows in the country, the road system is slowly being improved. In addition, even a bus ride the length or width of the country lasts only a few hours. And of course, it is on inexpensive buses, not planes, that you'll have the opportunity to meet local Belizeans on their way to market or from one town to another.

Geography

Belize is a lush, tropical country. It is best known for the 200-mile-long (320-kilometer-long) string of cayes, or coral islands, that stretch the length of the country a few miles offshore. The islands are the above-water part of a barrier reef second in extent only to Australia's Great Barrier Reef.

Belize's mainland is less than 200 miles (320 kilometers) long, and 75 miles (120 kilometers) wide at its widest point, yet its geography ranges from true lowland rainforest to pleasant highland plateaus and mountains. The northern half of the country is primarily flat. Sprawling mangrove swamps blur the distinction between open sea and true coast. Inland, most of the north is covered by dense hardwood forests, save where farmers have cleared land to grow sugar and other crops near the Mexican border.

Central Belize is an area of hills and valleys. It is here the ancient Mayans lived and worked their crops. Belmopan, the still-developing capital of Belize, lies beside the Belize River in the central part of the country. The ruins of one of the Mayans' major ceremonial centers, Xunantunich, lie up-river from Belmopan near the Guatemalan border. Farther inland, across the border in Guatemala, lie the famous Mayan ruins of Tikal, which may be reached by road from Belize. (You'll need a passport and a pre-arranged visa or tourist card to get into Guatemala. There is no Guatemalan consulate in Belize.)

From central Belize, the Maya Mountains rise to the south. At 3,681 feet (1,122 meters), Victoria Peak is the highest point in the Mayas and in the country. The Mayas climb sharply from the southern coastal area, where almost continuous rain creates true rainforest conditions. The southern Belize rainforest is covered with thick, lush stands of palms and ferns. Short rivers run down from the Mayas through this wet, steamy area.

Climate

Belize has two seasons, rainy and dry. The dry season more or less coincides with winter in North America, running from December or January to May or June. Divers prefer visiting the country in late spring, when the coastal waters around the reefs are clearest. Other visitors prefer the cooler temperatures of the early part of the dry season. The rainy season begins in May or June. By November, the rainy season tapers off, and by January, northern Belize has often turned dry and dusty.

Northern Belize receives about 60 inches (150 centimeters) of rain per year. In the southern rainforests, where the rainy season continues year round except for a slight reprieve from February to April, about 150 inches (380 centimeters) of rain fall each year.

Belize's weather is humid and hot from March to September, when temperatures in Belize City range in the 80s and 90s (30s centigrade) during the day and cool off to the 70s (20s centigrade) at night. It is appreciably cooler from November to March, when high temperatures in Belize City reach only into the 70s (20s centigrade).

Adventure-Travel Possibilities

The most popular destination among visitors to Belize is the country's **coral reef and cayes (1)**. The string of coral islands offers tropical paradise at a fraction of the cost of the West Indies. If you desire, there are plenty of nice—and expensive—resorts on the two largest and most developed cayes—Ambergris and Caulker. If you want to rough it a little, there are many rustic resorts on both the larger and the smaller cayes. There are also deserted cayes on which to camp all alone.

If you're coming from Mexico and your destination is Ambergris Caye, it is possible to fly to the town of San Pedro on Ambergris from Corozal, the northern Belizean town just across the border from Mexico. Most people, however, reach the cayes from Belize City on the central coast. Regular flights and ferries go to San Pedro, 35 miles (55 kilometers) distant. Regular ferries also go to Caye Caulker. Irregular ferries go to other cayes. In addition, private boats may be hired to reach the smallest, most tranquil cayes.

Because of its airstrip and the great diving and snorkeling just offshore, Ambergris is the most developed of the cayes. San Pedro is a delightful town of colorful wooden buildings, but the caye is fast going the way of other resplendent locations in neighboring Mexico that have been discovered by the tourist industry and overrun with resorts. Before the giant resorts come along, however, Ambergris is still a pleasant getaway, and San Pedro's bars and seafood restaurants are enjoyable.

For years, Caye Caulker has been a favorite destination of budget travelers. In keeping with the clientele, hotel and food prices are considerably lower than those of Ambergris. For example, diving gear and boat rental might set you back more than $100 per person on Ambergris, whereas groups commonly form to rent a small boat and snorkeling gear on Caye Caulker for a few dollars per person.

If you want to camp on a deserted caye or beach, you have only to ask around in Belize City to learn of a place suitable to you and to find a boat to take you there. Be sure to learn whether fresh water will be available. And since mosquitoes and sand fleas are residents of most of the cayes, remember to bring repellent.

In addition to sunning on palm-fringed beaches and diving and snorkeling around colorful coral reefs, fishing is justifiably popular off the cayes, since the area swarms with fish. Sport-fishing gear and deep-water boats with guides to go after large fish may be rented for about $200 per day. The shallow lagoon surrounded by the low-lying **Turneffe Islands (2)** is said to be the best place in the world to go after bonefish.

Even if the cayes are your main destination, be sure to build in some extra time, if possible, to explore mainland Belize. Since the country is small, it is possible to do much, even of a backcountry nature, in a short period of time. A two-week vacation is ample time to visit one of the cayes for a few days and to explore the Belizean mainland before heading home, even if you fly in and out of Cancun on a low-cost fare to save money. Rental cars and jeeps are available in Belize City, but they're not cheap. Buses run regularly on all the main highways, while communal taxis go to outlying population centers.

Southwest of Belize City and Belmopan is **Mountain Pine Ridge Reserve (3)**. The reserve is a long, pine-covered ridge on the edge of the Maya Mountains that is reminiscent of areas far to the north. Streams, caves and waterfalls are plentiful, including 1,800-foot (550-meter) Hidden Valley Falls, highest in Central America. Although no overnight camping is allowed in the reserve, hiking is popular and horses are available for hire.

The **San Ignacio-Benque Viejo area (4)** west of the reserve near the Guatemalan border offers a good base from which to explore Mountain Pine Ridge as well as the impressive Xunantunich ruins and the tropical jungle that surrounds them. San Ignacio, a sleepy, Spanish-flavored town also known as Cayo, has several decent hotels and lodges, including the Jamal Ranch Cottages, run by a North American couple. Guests stay in Mayan-style thatched cottages on the 150-acre ranch. Camping facilities are available, too. The couple offers guided tours of Mountain Pine Ridge and Xunantunich. They also have horses for hire to explore the surrounding area, and canoes for rent to float down the peaceful Macal River. From such a base it would be possible to spend several relaxing days—if not a lifetime.

Those who want to get a taste of the real wilds of Belize must head south into the rainforest from Belize City. To experience the rainforest on an established trail, go as far south as you can, to the end of the Southern Highway at the colorful Indian villages of **San Pedro Colombia and San Antonio (5)**. From the end of the road at San Antonio, a well-established footpath takes traders through the jungle and on into Guatemala. The path is an excellent way to experience the tropical flora and fauna of southern Belize, since the vegetation is too thick to allow you to dive directly into the wilderness.

Of note in the area: the Mayan ruins of Lubaantan are on the outskirts of San Pedro, and travelers on extended journeys can enter Guatemala and Honduras by ferry from Punta Gorda.

Like most Central American countries, Belize is home to a wide variety of bird species. The swampy coastal area in the north has been called a paradise by bird-watchers. About 30 miles (20 kilometers) north of Belize City off the Northern Highway, the Belize Audubon Society operates the 3,000-acre **Crooked Tree Wildlife Refuge (6)**.

Information Sources

Much of Belize's allure is based on the fact that the country hasn't been visited much by tourists. For the most part, that is great news for the backcountry enthusiast. However, it also means that, until recently, guidebooks on Belize were scarce. Only two guidebooks cover Belize exclusively, but both are excellent. One, *Belize Guide* (Passport Press), is written by Paul Glassman, a resident of Central America. Glassman knows what facts every traveler needs to know, and he includes them in his guide. His thoughtful descriptions of the people and places of Belize fill out the guide exceedingly well.

The other book on Belize is the *Belize Handbook* (Moon Publications) by Chicki Mallan. Mallan does as fine a job of offering information on outdoor activities in Belize as she does in her *Guide to the Yucatan Peninsula*.

For those who will be traveling to Belize on a budget, Glassman and Mallan offer some information on low-priced lodging and food. More information for the budget traveler is provided in the short chapter on Belize in Geoff Crowther's *South America on a Shoestring* (Lonely Planet Publications).

Another book for budget travelers concentrates on Belize and neighboring Guatemala. *Guatemala and Belize: The Real Guide* (Prentice Hall Press) follows the tradition begun by the publisher of the *Mexico and Central American Handbook*. The book provides detailed information on lodging and restaurants in Belize, as well as information on outdoor activities in the country.

Backpacking in Mexico and Central America (Bradt Publications), by Hilary Bradt and Rob Rachowiecki, includes several pages of information on backcountry possibilities in Belize. The cayes and Mountain Pine Ridge Reserve are covered.

For an advance look at Belize, watch the movie adaptation of novelist and travel writer Paul Theroux's novel, *The Mosquito Coast* (available on videotape), which was filmed in the country. The movie captures the lushness of Belize's jungles and the easygoing Caribbean nature of its people.

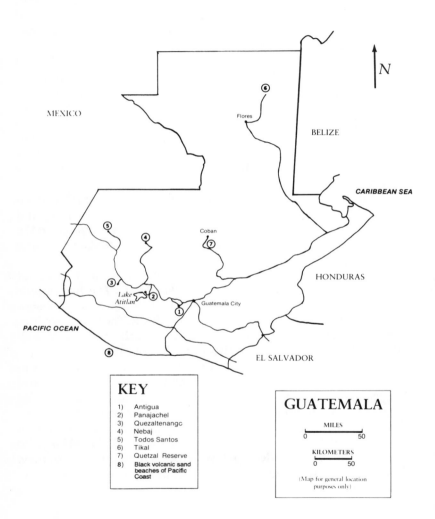

MEXICO

BELIZE

Flores ⑥

CARIBBEAN SEA

Coban
⑤   ⑦
    ④
HONDURAS

③ *Lake Atitlan* ②
① Guatemala City

PACIFIC OCEAN

⑧

EL SALVADOR

N

KEY

1) Antigua
2) Panajachel
3) Quezaltenango
4) Nebaj
5) Todos Santos
6) Tikal
7) Quetzal Reserve
8) Black volcanic sand
   beaches of Pacific
   Coast

GUATEMALA

MILES

0   50

KILOMETERS

0   50

(Map for general location
purposes only)

Chapter 8

Guatemala

Overview

For the adventurous traveler, Guatemala offers the opportunity to combine a backcountry trek with the color and spice of the Mayan Indian culture still alive today. Trails wind throughout the country's highlands and to the top of still-rumbling volcanoes. Visitors to Guatemala, which straddles the Central American isthmus south of Mexico, generally arrive by plane, although the country may be reached by road from the United States and Canada via Mexico. Once in Guatemala, visitors may choose local buses, rental cars or plane flights for travel from Guatemala City, the modern capital with nearly a million inhabitants, to the highlands and other parts of the country. Travel in the country is inexpensive, even by Latin American standards.

The colonial town of Antigua, the former capital, is a quiet, beautiful base from which to set out on backcountry hikes. Antigua is tucked in the mountains only 40 miles (65 kilometers) from Guatemala City. From Antigua, trails snake into the mountains. Some lead to the top of nearby volcanoes.

Author Aldous Huxley called Lake Atitlan, nestled in the highlands 90 miles (150 kilometers) from Guatemala City, the most beautiful lake on earth. The town of Panajachel on the shores of Atitlan is another good base from which to explore the highland backcountry.

Until quite recently, simply visiting Guatemala would have been considered an adventurous travel act of the first magnitude. For much of the 1980s, the country's repressive military regime was locked in a bloody struggle with guerrilla groups whose ranks were made up of landless, poverty-stricken campesinos tired of being controlled by the country's ruling class. The situation was the worst that Latin American politics can offer. It destroyed Guatemala's tourism industry, which had just begun to flourish in the 1970s.

In the last few years the conflict in Guatemala has calmed, and tourists have begun to return. Today, Guatemala is fast regaining its reputation among visitors as one of the most diverse and delightful destinations in Latin America.

The Mayan culture that thrived throughout the region for well over a thousand years, from before the time of Christ until the arrival of the Spanish in 1523, is still very much alive in Guatemala today. Fully 50 percent of the citizens of the country are full-blooded Indians—the highest percentage in Central America. Called *indigenas*, they are direct descendants of the various Mayan tribes that populated present-day Guatemala.

Most of Guatemala's Indians continue to follow the subsistence farming, weaving and pottery-making ways of their Mayan forebears. Many still wear the distinctive, colorful tribal clothing that differentiated the various Mayan groups in earlier centuries. Each clothing style incorporates a startlingly bright symbol or geometric pattern unique to a particular village. The *indigenas* live in isolated villages in the rugged, verdant highlands of central and southern Guatemala. As visitors to the backcountry hike from one highland Indian village to another, they encounter in each a style and design of dress, from shoes to headgear, that has been unique to that village for centuries. In many cases, the dialect spoken by the people of a particular village is unique as well.

To this day, the various Indian groups maintain their independence from one another as well as from the Guatemalan government. Their religion, though outwardly labelled Catholicism to appease the conquering Spanish, retains many elements of the Mayan religion of their ancestors. Despite their fierce independence, the *indigenas* are accommodating to visitors, who buy the high-quality weavings, clothing and pottery the Indians produce.

In addition to the *indigenas,* 40 percent of Guatemala's population are *ladinos*—those of mixed Indian and European heritage or of pure European heritage. They live in the cities and larger towns of Guatemala, speak Spanish, wear European-style clothing and control most of the country's wealth. On the coasts are sizeable populations of black Africans, who were brought to Guatemala from throughout the West Indies to work the country's coastal banana plantations. Guatemala's remote Caribbean coast is also home to the Carib Indians. The Caribs are the descendants of a tribe of native Middle American Indians who came to the coast of Guatemala and intermarried with escaped slaves living there. The result is a people predominantly African in race but Indian in culture.

Many visitors to Guatemala are attracted by the country's tremendous cultural diversity—especially the continued diversity and independence of the tribes that made up the Mayan civilization until little more than 300 years ago. The country's cultural richness combined with hiking, backpacking, volcano climbing and bicycling, and the opportunity to explore the shores of two oceans, makes Guatemala one of the best adventure-travel destinations in Latin America today.

Geography

Guatemala stretches the width of the Central American isthmus, from the Pacific Ocean in the southwest to the Caribbean Sea in the northeast. It sits directly south of Mexico and the tiny country of Belize. Honduras and El Salvador border Guatemala on the southeast.

Guatemala is little larger than the state of Ohio, yet it contains in its 42,000 square miles (110,000 square kilometers) a wide variety of geographical features, from mountain ranges and active volcanoes reaching nearly 14,000 feet (4,250 meters) in height to the steaming Peten jungle in the north, whose thick overgrowth hides so many Mayan ruins that new finds are still occasionally reported today.

The country's major distinguishing feature is the Sierra Madre, a mountain range running west to east across the country. South of the Sierra Madre is a chain of nearly 30 volcanoes running parallel to the Pacific coast. Most of Guatemala's 8 million citizens live in the highlands. At one time, the highlands were covered by forest. Today, much of the highlands have been cleared to make way for the cultivation of corn to feed Guatemala's steadily growing populace. Still, the highlands are a beautiful region of quiet villages in deep valleys separated by high mountain ridges. The villages are connected by footpaths worn smooth by centuries of use, and these provide perfect routes for backpackers.

South of the mountains lie the fertile, hot Pacific lowlands. North of the highlands is the Peten jungle, location of Tikal and many other Mayan ruins. This region is being cleared and settled today, as Guatemala's burgeoning population forces the development of previously untouched wilderness. With settlement has come the rapid deforestation of the Peten's age-old hardwood forests to make room for farms and ranches.

The highlands of northeastern Guatemala slope gently down to Lake Izbal, the largest lake in Guatemala, and on down to the moist Caribbean lowlands, a region of rainforests interspersed with banana plantations.

Climate

Guatemala is far enough north of the equator that temperatures rise and dip noticeably from season to season. However, the primary seasonal correlate, as in much of equatorial Latin America, is rain. When it rains, it rains hard in Guatemala. The rainy season is from May to October.

The best months to visit Guatemala are November and December. During those months, just after the rains have ended, the mountains and jungles are alive with wildflowers (including Guatemala's more than 100 orchid species), the rivers and streams are full, and temperatures in the highlands are crisp but not cold. January and February are fine months for visiting as well. It's a little cooler in the highlands during those months, but it never gets too cold in Guatemala—all you'll need to stay warm in mid-winter are a sweater and a light jacket.

The last months of the dry season, March and April, are less than ideal. After several months without rain, the Guatemalan countryside begins to look parched. Dust is often chokingly thick on roads and trails, and views are often obscured by a haze of smoke as farmers burn their fields in preparation for the coming growing season.

Adventure-Travel Possibilities

The most popular adventure-travel activities in Guatemala are hiking, backpacking and volcano climbing in the highlands. Unlike in North America's large, uninhabited wilderness areas, you can expect to hike for no more than few minutes between settled plots of land in the densely populated Guatemalan highlands. However, the cultural richness and diversity of the many highland Indians you meet make a walk in roadless areas of rural Guatemala rewarding.

As you walk, you'll be greeted by Indians in a variety of ethnic costumes. In backcountry villages, you'll be the object of polite

attention. You'll be welcome to camp where you like—near a
village or in the countryside between villages—with permission of
the locals. Once you're away from Guatemala City, virtually all the
highlands offer prime country for day hiking and backpacking.
Some possible starting points follow.

Antigua (1): The former capital of Spain's Central American
territories is today a quiet town popular with tourists. The capital
was destroyed twice by earthquakes and floods, once in 1541 and
again in 1773. After the second catastrophe, the capital was moved
40 miles (65 kilometers) to the site of present-day Guatemala City
at the edge of the highlands. Santiago de los Caballeros, as Antigua
was then known, was left to decay. In the 19th century, however,
it became an agricultural center for the cultivation of coffee. Old
colonial mansions were restored and reoccupied, as were government buildings. Over time, Santiago became known as Antigua
Guatemala, or Old Guatemala. Today, the colonial gem set in
green, flower-bedecked hills is known simply as Antigua.

As a living colonial monument, Antigua is a regular stop on all
tour itineraries. The town is especially well known for its colorful
Holy Week processions, which pass over carpets of fresh flowers
woven on the streets of town each night throughout the week.

Many visitors stay in Antigua for weeks or months at a time to
study Spanish. Courses that include room and board with a local
family and several hours of instruction each day are available for
as little as $300 a month.

Day hikes into the hills surrounding Antigua are popular, as are
climbs of three nearby volcanoes, the highest of which, Acatenango, is the third highest peak in Guatemala at just over 13,000 feet
(4,000 meters). The easiest climb of the three is 12,300-foot (3,750-
meter) Volcan de Agua—a dirt road leads all the way to a radio
tower at its summit. Acatenango may be attempted as a long day
climb. However, if you want to climb nearby Volcan de Fuego on
the same expedition, you'll need to carry enough gear and water
to spend a night between the two summits. Acatenango is 700 feet
(210 meters) higher than Fuego ("fire"). Those who climb the aptly
named peak are sometimes rewarded with views of red lava and
spurts of cinders, steam and smoke from Fuego's crater, since the
volcano is still intermittently active.

Panajachel (2): This town of less than 4,000 people is the main
tourist base for visits to Lake Atitlan, 90 miles (150 kilometers) from

Guatemala City. The town consists primarily of tourist hotels and restaurants. It is so popular with foreigners that it is known in Guatemala as "Gringo-tenango." Panajachel is a comfortable base from which to explore the lake and the dozen traditional Indian villages that line its shore. The *indigenas* of these villages are said to be the most colorfully dressed of all Guatemala's Indians.

Visitors may walk the roughly 35 miles (55 kilometers) around Lake Atitlan, camping along the way, or hike into the hills above the lake. Atitlan, Toliman and San Pedro, the three towering volcanoes that provide Lake Atitlan's famous scenic backdrop to the south, are all popular climbs. The highest of the three, 11,500-foot (3,500-meter) Atitlan, is a tough climb through heavy underbrush requiring an overnight camp en route.

Quezaltenango (3): With a population of more than 60,000, Quezaltenango is the largest city in the highlands and the second largest in Guatemala after Guatemala City. In the late 19th century, Quezaltenango rivaled Guatemala City as the most important commercial center in the country. Then, in 1902, an earthquake levelled much of the city. Quezaltenango was slow to recover from the devastating quake. The city no longer rivals Guatemala City in size or importance, but it remains the center of trade and commerce for the highlands.

At more than 7,500 feet (2,300 meters), Quezaltenango is a high, cool city surrounded by nearby peaks, including the cone of Santa Maria Volcano. Quezaltenango's colorful daily market, with Indian merchants from throughout the region, is popular with visitors. Day hikes in the area allow visits to smaller Indian villages. However, the two most popular day hikes in the area lead not to villages but to the summits of Santa Maria and the highest peak in all of Central America—13,845-foot (4,220-meter) Tajumulco.

The 12,375-foot (3,772-meter) summit of Santa Maria is a three- to four-hour hike from the trailhead 3 miles (5 kilometers) outside Quezaltenango. Tajumulco is a four- to five-hour climb above the town of Tuchan near Quezaltenango. Although the volcano can easily be climbed in a day, many parties choose to bring gear and water to spend the night on the summit. From the top of Tajumulco are clear dawn views of Guatemala's mountains and its chain of volcanoes falling away to the Pacific Ocean.

After hiking and climbing in the Quezaltenango area, you may wish to avail yourself to the comforts of one of the several hot springs baths in the area.

Nebaj (4): The remote highland town of Nebaj is a long day's journey over rough roads by bus from Guatemala City. It is little visited by foreigners. As a result, the town has a feeling of tradition and charm lacking in the more tourist-oriented towns of the highlands closer to Guatemala City.

The trip to Nebaj is worthwhile simply to see the women of the town, whose red-and-white layered blouses, red skirts and cloth head wraps won the native costume competition in the Miss Universe pageant several years ago. Day hikes in the hills surrounding Nebaj include the walk over a ridge to the alpine valley hamlet of Acul. An overnight walk extends from Nebaj to Cunen.

Todos Santos (5): Since the men of Nebaj no longer wear their traditional dress, you'll have to go elsewhere to see just how fancied up the men of Guatemala's highlands can get. One such place is Todos Santos. The men of Todos Santos sport striped shirts with long, embroidered collars, white trousers with wool overpants to warm the hips, and leather sandals with large heel cups.

A two- to four-day hike leads from the end of the road at Todos Santos, over a pass and down to the villages of San Juan Atitan, Santiago Chimaltenango and San Pedro Necta. The Pan-American Highway can be reached in just a few hours from any of the three villages, enabling backpackers to end their hike when they wish and take public transport back to their starting point.

Bicycling is another good way to visit the highlands. Since private cars are not common outside Guatemala City and Quezaltenango, riders compete for road space only with buses and trucks—and with relatively few of them on roads other than the busy Pan-American Highway, which bisects the highlands. Mountain bikes are best, since they can be ridden on paved, gravel or dirt roads.

The single most popular travel destination in all of Guatemala is **Tikal (6).** The ruins of one of the greatest cities of the Mayan civilization lie deep in a protected area of the Peten jungle, 40 miles (65 kilometers) northeast of Flores in northern Guatemala. Flores is 16 to 24 hours by bus from Guatemala City. Most visitors fly to Flores (about $40 each way) and continue on to Tikal by bus from there. Tikal is also easily reached by road from Belize.

The Mayan civilization had a decentralized government. The government loosely controlled independent tribes that often warred with one another. Even so, together the tribes financed and built huge cities and temple complexes throughout what is today Honduras, Guatemala, Belize and southern Mexico. Today those ruins—including Tikal—are popular tourist attractions.

Because Tikal is set in a national park, it is wonderful to visit, to experience both the ancient city and the unspoiled jungle that surrounds it. Camping at Tikal is allowed, and it is recommended because the ruins are magical at night, with the moon breaking through the clouds and jungle noises sounding hauntingly near.

You may wish to backpack from Tikal 15 miles (25 kilometers) along the deserted jeep track that connects Tikal to the Uaxactun ruins deep in the Peten. The Uaxactun ruins aren't as extensive nor the pyramids as tall as those of Tikal, but you'll have the place to yourself, away from the fly-in, fly-out tours that at times besiege Tikal.

The *Biotopo del Quetzal,* or **Quetzal Reserve (7),** a little more than 100 miles (160 kilometers) north of Guatemala City on the road to Coban, is popular with birders. Nature trails wind through the high rainforest protected by the reserve. Sightings of the rare quetzal, with its brilliant green and red markings and long, streaming tail feathers, are possible. The quetzal is the national bird of Guatemala.

After exploring Guatemala's highlands and jungle, you may want to spend some time relaxing on the coast. If so, the direction to head is south, to the **black volcanic sand beaches of the Pacific Coast (8).** Guatemala boasts some of the most beautiful and least developed beaches in Latin America. They're fine for those who relish privacy, but accommodations and restaurants are rare. Since only rough beach huts are available for lodging, many visitors visit the coast in a long day from Guatemala City.

Information Sources

The best guide to hiking, backpacking and volcano climbing in Guatemala is *Backpacking in Mexico and Central America* by Hilary Bradt and Rob Rachowiecki (Bradt Publications). The book has a detailed chapter on Guatemala that describes several volcano climbs and backpacking trips. The authors stress, however, that their backpacking trail descriptions are only a start. "Although we give some specific trails to inspire confidence, you can hike anywhere," they write. "Really, the scope is endless." Reports one

Guatemala: "Hiking in Guatemala is without doubt the best I've ever done...an enthralling experience."

Backpacking and Camping in Mexico and Central America may be teamed up with Paul Glassman's superb *Guatemala Guide* (Passport Press). Like his guides to Belize and Costa Rica, Glassman's guide to Guatemala is exhaustively researched and interesting to read. In addition to providing a good historical, geographical and cultural overview of Guatemala, Glassman offers hotel, restaurant and travel information for the entire country.

As it does for Belize, *Guatemala and Belize: The Real Guide* (Prentice Hall Press) provides detailed information for independent travelers to Guatemala, including descriptions of volcano climbs and other backcountry pursuits in the country.

J.P. Panet, author of *Latin America on Bicycle* (Passport Press), includes a chapter chronicling his two-week mountain bike trip through the Guatemalan highlands.

If you'll be spending a few days in and around Antigua, you may want to buy Mike Shawcross' *Antigua, Guatemala: City and Area Guide,* available in town.

N

CARIBBEAN SEA

⑥

⑤

Tela   La Ceiba

San Pedro Sula

GUATEMALA

④   ③

②

①

Tegucigalpa

EL SALVADOR   NICARAGUA

PACIFIC OCEAN

KEY

1) La Tigra National Park
2) Gracias
3) Santa Rosa de Copan
4) Copan
5) Coastal trails
6) Bay Islands

HONDURAS

MILES

0   100

KILOMETERS

0   100

(Map for general location
purposes only)

Chapter 9

Honduras

Overview

Honduras is little visited by tourists, yet it presents intriguing possibilities to the adventurous traveler. The country boasts several tourist gems, including the tropical Gulf coast, the Mayan ruins at Copan, the Bay Islands in the Caribbean, and La Tigra National Park. Except for the Bay Islands, where lodging is expensive by Latin American standards, travel in Honduras is inexpensive.

Although scattered guerrilla activity has taken place in the country, it is Honduras' pervasive poverty that most accounts for its lack of foreign visitors. The country has become even poorer because of the refugee burden it has assumed in recent years. Displaced citizens and out-of-work soldiers have poured into Honduras to escape wars that have been or are being fought in all three of its neighboring countries—Guatemala to the northwest, El Salvador to the southwest and Nicaragua to the east.

As a result of its grinding poverty, Honduras is little developed. Few roads in the country are paved; many are not even graveled. The Honduran national park system includes only one park, which has minimal facilities for visitors. Subsistence farming is the norm in Honduras, where much of the population wrests a hand-to-mouth existence from small plots of land scattered throughout the western highlands.

Fully 90 percent of Hondurans are *mestizo*—of mixed Indian and Spanish heritage. On the Gulf coast live blacks whose ancestors were brought to the mainland from various Caribbean islands to cultivate and harvest bananas. Just off the Gulf coast are the Honduran Bay Islands. The islands once served as hideouts for

European buccaneers preying on the conquistadors' booty being hauled by ship from the Americas to Spain. Today, light-skinned, English-speaking descendants of the buccaneers still inhabit the islands, along with blacks, Indians and a growing number of *mestizos* from the mainland.

Present-day Honduras was once part of the Mayan empire. It was settled by the Spanish in the 1500s. The country declared independence from Spain in 1821. Soon after, it joined the federation known as the United Provinces of Central America. The federation collapsed in 1838. The country has been ruled since by a series of military juntas and autocratic civilian governments.

Tegucigalpa, the capital of Honduras, and San Pedro Sula, the second largest city after Tegucigalpa, can be reached by air from the United States. The country can also be reached overland from the United States via Mexico and Guatemala. Once in Honduras, visitors can travel by bus, plane or rental car. Ferries and planes take visitors from the mainland to the Bay Islands.

Geography

Honduras stretches across the Central American isthmus southeast of Guatemala and west of Nicaragua. Honduras is the second largest country in Central America after Nicaragua. With an area of 43,300 square miles (112,000 square kilometers), it is slightly larger than Tennessee. Western Honduras is a high, rugged land of heavily forested mountains and deep valleys. By contrast, eastern Honduras is a flat, low-lying region of dense rainforests.

Climate

Although Honduras is hot and tropical like the rest of Central America, visitors to the country will get some relief because most of their time will likely be spent in the populous western highlands, where temperatures are cooler.

The rainy season in the highlands generally starts in May and lasts until November. From late December until April, temperatures are warm and skies are generally clear.

Rain falls on the Gulf coast all year long. The months with the least precipitation are March, April and May.

Adventure-Travel Possibilities

La Tigra National Park (1) protects a fragile area of dense forest less than 20 miles (30 kilometers) northeast of Tegucigalpa. Old roads stretching throughout La Tigra that once linked mining towns in the area now may be followed by hikers. The roads wind through the steep, cloud-enshrouded mountains of the park, which harbors trees, wildflowers, and a variety of bird and animal life.

Several Spanish colonial towns in the highlands are popular with visitors. Two of those towns, **Gracias (2)** and **Santa Rosa de Copan (3)** are good bases for day hikes and backpacking trips into the surrounding mountains. From Gracias, a series of trails used by locals cuts across the northern flank of the highest mountain in Honduras, 9,348-foot (2,849-meter) Celaque, also known as Las Minas. These trails are ideal for backpacking. Day hikers may walk 5 miles from Gracias to El Presidente hot springs for a relaxing soak before heading back to town.

West of Santa Rosa de Copan on the Guatemalan border are the extensive Mayan ruins of **Copan (4)**. The ruins have been cleared of jungle overgrowth, and some temples and pyramids have been reconstructed. Guides are available at the ruins.

The Gulf coast of Honduras is threaded by trails used by the friendly locals of the region. Many of the trails link roadless coastal villages. The **50-mile (80-kilometer) stretch of coastal trails (5)** linking Tela in the west, La Ceiba in the east and numerous coastal villages between is perfect for backpackers. Tela and La Ceiba are connected by an inland road, so the walk may be done in either direction.

The **Bay Islands (6)** off the Gulf coast are great for relaxing, swimming, snorkeling and diving. Dive resorts on the three main islands—Utila, Roatan and Guanaja—are popular with North American visitors. The Bay Islands may be reached by plane from San Pedro Sula or by ferry from La Ceiba.

Information Sources

Backpacking in Mexico and Central America (Bradt Publications) provides a good deal of information on backcountry possibilities in Honduras. In addition to general information on Honduras, the book covers La Tigra National Park, highlands hikes and the walk on the Gulf coast between Tela and La Ceiba.

South America on a Shoestring (Lonely Planet Publications) offers a few pages of general where-to-stay, how-to-get-around information on Honduras. Included are the Bay Islands and the Copan ruins.

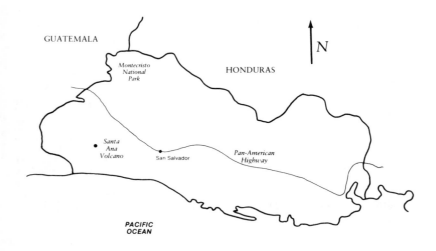

GUATEMALA

Montecristo National Park

HONDURAS

Santa Ana Volcano

San Salvador

Pan-American Highway

N

PACIFIC
OCEAN

EL SALVADOR

MILES

0	50

KILOMETERS

0	50

(Map for general location
purposes only)

Chapter 10

El Salvador

Overview

The civil war that has torn El Salvador apart since the 1970s continues today, making backcountry travel in the country impossible. Leftist guerrillas operating in the country's rural areas continue their insurgency against El Salvador's right-wing government. In retaliation, government security forces indiscriminately torture and murder citizens suspected of consorting with the rebels. Amnesty International has repeatedly condemned the El Salvadoran government for its death squads, but money continues to pour into the government's coffers from the United States—to date, El Salvador has received more than $3 billion in foreign aid from the U.S. government.

Although the Pan-American Highway runs through El Salvador between Guatemala and Honduras, few travelers are foolish enough to follow its route these days. Instead, travelers going overland through Central America bypass El Salvador via the rough roads that connect Guatemala and Honduras directly.

El Salvador is a small, densely populated country. The country is smaller than the state of Vermont, yet it has a Spanish-Indian population of 5 million people—ten times more than the half million people who live in Vermont. The capital of El Salvador is San Salvador.

El Salvadorans are notable for their stoicism in the face of harsh poverty and, since long before the start of the civil war, brutal government repression. Throughout the 1960s and early 1970s, El Salvador's welcoming citizens and gorgeous Pacific beaches made the country a favorite stop on the "gringo trail"—the overland route followed by young travelers through Central and South America. Perhaps it will one day be so again.

Geography

El Salvador is the smallest country in Central America, with a land mass of a little more than 8,000 square miles (20,000 square kilometers). It is tucked against the Pacific side of the Central American isthmus. Honduras borders El Salvador on the north and east; Guatemala borders the country on the west.

El Salvador is a verdant land of mountains, valleys and volcanoes. It has been one of the world's leading coffee exporters since the discovery, in the late 1800s, that the layer of volcanic soil that covers much of El Salvador combined with the abundant rainfall made El Salvador perfect for coffee cultivation.

Climate

El Salvador's tropical climate repeats that of the rest of Central America. Summers are hot, muggy and rainy. Winters are slightly cooler and skies are generally clear.

Adventure-Travel Possibilities

Little virgin forest remains in El Salvador. Instead, most of the land has been cleared for cultivation and cattle grazing. Only on the steep flanks of El Salvador's mountains and volcanoes do patches of old-growth forest remain.

El Salvador's limited backcountry areas have been the scene of much fighting during the civil war, so it is hard to say what shape they will be in when the war finally ends. Before the war, the government was doing an admirable job of developing a system of small national parks protecting the country's remaining natural areas. Perhaps those areas will still be worth exploring when El Salvador is once again safe for visitors.

The largest of these parks is Montecristo National Park, which protects a large section of cloud forest—an area of perpetual clouds and rain—in the extreme northwest corner of the country. Three volcanoes in western El Salvador, including Santa Ana, the highest point in the country at 7,724 feet (2,354 meters), were popular climbs before the war.

Information Sources

Geoff Crowther's *South America on a Shoestring* (Lonely Planet Publications) provides a few pages of basic information on El

Salvador. *Backpacking in Mexico and Central America* (Bradt Publications) offers a concise description of the hiking and climbing possible in El Salvador before the war.

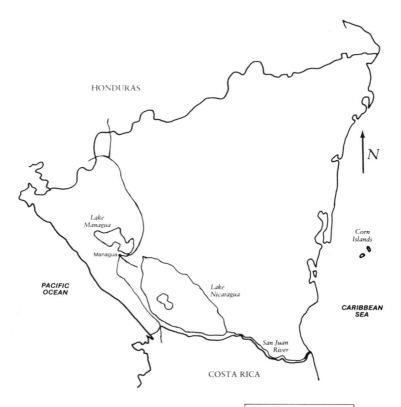

HONDURAS

N

Lake
Managua

Managua

PACIFIC
OCEAN

Lake
Nicaragua

Corn
Islands

CARIBBEAN
SEA

San Juan
River

COSTA RICA

NICARAGUA

MILES
0   50

KILOMETERS
0   50

(Map for general location
purposes only)

Chapter 11

Nicaragua

Overview

Political unrest has made Nicaragua's backcountry off-limits to travelers since the civil war in the late 1970s that resulted in a dramatic change of government—from the U.S.-backed, right-wing Somoza dictatorship to the socialist government of the revolutionary Sandinista party.

After defeating the Somoza government and coming to power in 1979, the Sandinistas faced battles on two fronts. They fought to replace the repressive, centralized Somoza regime with a socialist order involving all Nicaraguans. At the same time, the Sandinistas were fighting the right-wing Contra army based across the border from Nicaragua in Honduras. The Contras waged a guerrilla war against the government throughout much of the 1980s with the open financial support of the U.S. government.

Not until President Ronald Reagan left office in 1989 did direct U.S. military aid to the Contras end. The end to that aid meant the end to the Contras as an effective guerrilla force. Still, it hasn't been long since much of Nicaragua's backcountry was the scene of fierce battles. As a result, Nicaragua's backcountry is still considered off-limits by prudent travelers.

For now, travel in populated areas of Nicaragua is considered safe for visitors. Indeed, throughout the 1980s, as the U.S.-backed Contras battled with the government troops, Nicaragua was a popular destination for U.S. citizens who helped with crop harvests and construction projects as a show of support for the Nicaraguan people. Such volunteer efforts are still popular today.

Geography

Nicaragua is both the largest country in Central America and the one with the lowest population density. With an area of 49,600 square miles (128,500 square kilometers), Nicaragua is roughly the size of Pennsylvania. The country spans the Central American isthmus. It is bordered on the north by Honduras and on the south by Costa Rica. Most of Nicaragua's nearly 3 million people live in the fertile stretch of lowlands near the Pacific coast. The two largest lakes in Central America, Lake Nicaragua and Lake Managua, separate the Pacific lowlands from the dense, little explored rainforests of Nicaragua's Gulf of Mexico drainage.

Nicaragua is a low-lying country of rainforests and farmland broken only by isolated mountains in the north-central region of the country near the Honduran border, and a spectacular chain of peaks, including some active volcanoes, that runs parallel to the Pacific coastline from the Gulf of Fonseca in the north to Lake Managua in the south.

Climate

Because most of Nicaragua lies just above sea level, the country is notable for its overwhelming heat and humidity. Summers are especially hot and sticky. The rainy season coincides with the summer months as well. The best time to visit Nicaragua is during winter, when temperatures aren't quite so oppressive and rain is less likely. The harvest season, when most volunteers visit, is from January to March.

Adventure-Travel Possibilities

The string of volcanoes that runs from north of Managua, the capital, to the Honduran border is the most accessible backcountry area in Nicaragua. If any backcountry region could be considered safe for exploration today, it is this area. In particular, Santiago Volcano National Park, only 40 minutes from Managua by bus, makes a good day visit. A paved road leads to the rim of this 2,000-foot-high (600-meter-high), active volcano. There are ample day-hiking possibilities in the area.

Other areas will perhaps be open to exploration by visitors in the years ahead. They include the isolated mountains of north-central Nicaragua, the remote Corn Islands off the Gulf coast, and the area encompassing the rugged trans-Nicaragua journey across Lake

Nicaragua and down the San Juan River to the Gulf coast, whence Costa Rica may be entered by hiking along the beach.

Information Sources

Backpacking in Mexico and Central America (Bradt Publications), by Hilary Bradt and Rob Rachowiecki, offers plenty of information on exploring Nicaragua's backcountry, including descriptions of volcano climbs near Managua and an account of the trans-Nicaragua journey mentioned above.

South America on a Shoestring (Lonely Planet Publications) provides several pages of information on travel and accommodations in populated parts of Nicaragua.

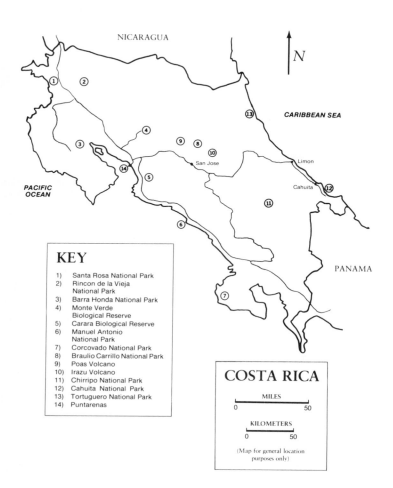

NICARAGUA

N

CARIBBEAN SEA

① ②

⑬

④

⑨ ⑧

⑩

San Jose

Limon

③

⑭

⑤

Cahuita

PACIFIC
OCEAN

⑪

⑫

⑥

KEY

1) Santa Rosa National Park
2) Rincon de la Vieja
   National Park
3) Barra Honda National Park
4) Monte Verde
   Biological Reserve
5) Carara Biological Reserve
6) Manuel Antonio
   National Park
7) Corcovado National Park
8) Braulio Carrillo National Park
9) Poas Volcano
10) Irazu Volcano
11) Chirripo National Park
12) Cahuita National Park
13) Tortuguero National Park
14) Puntarenas

⑦

PANAMA

COSTA RICA

MILES

0   50

KILOMETERS

0   50

(Map for general location
purposes only)

Chapter 12

Costa Rica

Overview

For the outdoors enthusiast willing to forego cultural sights in return for a chance to explore some of the best-preserved tropical wilderness on earth—and a chance to relax on some of the finest and most affordable tropical beaches found anywhere—Costa Rica is a paradise.

Costa Rica is unique among Central American nations in that its population is made up almost entirely of *blancos*—people of pure Spanish or other European origin. After the Spanish conquistadors came to the region of the Central American isthmus that is now Costa Rica, virtually all the native Indians living there died of various diseases introduced by the Spaniards. The result is that colorful Indian villages, found throughout much of Central America, do not exist in Costa Rica.

Because few native Indians survived to be put to work as low-class laborers by the Spaniards after their arrival in the 1500s, the struggles that developed in later years between those groups in neighboring countries have not plagued Costa Rica. Instead, Costa Rica has developed a fairly uniform, middle-class society. Today, the country is the most prosperous in Central America. Costa Rica has a functioning, democratic governmental system, an adequate transportation infrastructure and a phone system that actually works. Costa Rica's strong educational system has resulted in a literacy rate that rivals that of the United States.

Best of all for those interested in the backcountry, since the 1960s Costa Rica has been developing a national-park system with financial and technical support from the World Wildlife Fund and the Conservation Foundation. Today, the country's national parks are comparable to those of the United States and Canada in scope and accessibility. Nearly 10 percent of Costa Rica's 19,652 square miles (50,899 square kilometers) of land—the size of Vermont and New Hampshire combined—is set aside as national parks. The strong conservation ethic responsible for the breadth of the country's park system comes from the grassroots of Costa Rica's well-educated society. The animal populations in the parks are not being decimated by poachers as are many endangered species in national parks of other developing countries.

Costa Rica is also refreshing in that it has no armed forces. Its army was abolished in 1948, after the ruling government tried to use the armed forces to retain power after losing an election, and the country has been without an army ever since. Costa Rica has a long history of democratic rule. The country formed a democratic government upon gaining its independence from Spain in 1821. Except for minor lapses, like the one in 1948, it has maintained its democracy since.

Despite its relative prosperity compared to the rest of Central America, per-capita income in Costa Rica is still less than $2,000. Ox carts are the main form of transportation in the highlands where auto roads have not penetrated. Buses often are just as crowded and uncomfortable as in other parts of Latin America, and internal plane flights are just as liable to sudden cancellation or long delay. In addition, as evidenced by its 17 official holidays each year along with additional unplanned ones, Costa Rica shares in the relaxed attitude that makes Latin America a pleasure to experience.

Costa Rica offers the adventure traveler the best of both worlds: its well-established infrastructure and stable democratic government make it safe and easy to visit, and its protected backcountry—both the highlands, topped by still-active volcanoes, and the lowland rainforests—offers months of exploration possibilities.

While it is possible to reach Costa Rica overland from North America, you'd have to pass through little-developed Honduras and war-torn Nicaragua to do so. Instead, most visitors arrive by plane in San Jose, the capital.

When deciding how to get around the country, you'll be faced with a range of choices. Rental vehicles are available. Internal flights are a popular means of avoiding a long, bumpy journey by road to a remote location, and they offer fine views of the verdant landscape. Narrow-gauge trains run from San Jose in the central valley to Puntarenas on the Pacific coast and to Limon on the Caribbean. While the trains are slower than buses, they wind

Once covered by jungle growth, serpents carved in stone greet visitors to the Mayan ruins of Chichen Itza on Mexico's Yucatan peninsula. Chichen Itza joins southern Mexico's Palenque, Guatemala's Tikal and Honduras' Copan as the most impressive ruins remaining from the Mayan civilization that once spread across southern Mexico and northern Central America. Credit: Mexican Tourist Office

A catamaran slices the waves near Loreto off the east coast of Mexico's Baja California peninsula. Sailing, windsurfing and sea kayaking are popular off Baja and throughout the Caribbean. Credit: Mexican Tourism Office

Water sports are not limited to Latin America's seas. Here, pleasure craft await sailors on central Mexico's Lake Valle del Bravo. Elsewhere, Latin American lakes and rivers are ideal for canoeing, windsurfing, kayaking and rafting. Credit: Mexican Tourism Office

Backcountry bridges in Latin America come in all shapes and styles. Here, a backpacker crosses a tributary of the Amazon River high in the Bolivian Andes. Credit: Susan Graham

Like this idyllic stretch of Costa Rican coastline, quiet beaches await travelers throughout Central America and the Caribbean. Credit: Costa Rican Tourism Office

The rugged stretch of Andes Mountains comprising the Lake District, which straddles the Argentina-Chile border, is criss-crossed by well-maintained hiking trails. Credit: Nolan Hester

Ruins found in Costa Rica, like this Catholic church, are more recent than those of the Mayan civilization found further north in Central America. The country's lack of ancient ruins is more than compensated by its many jungle, mountain and coastal national parks brimming with plant, bird, animal and sea life. Credit: Costa Rican Tourism Office

Chimborazo Volcano, the highest point in Ecuador at 20,702 feet (6,310 meters), rises above the country's verdant central valley. Chimborazo and several other Ecuadorian volcanoes are increasingly popular ascents for high-altitude climbers. Credit: Kevin Graham

The Mayas' Temple of the Inscriptions rises from the surrounding jungle in Mexico's mountainous Chiapas state. The temple is one of several impressive, excavated structures at Palenque ruins. Credit: Kevin Graham

Sitting on the floating reed island on Lake Titicaca that is her home, a Peruvian Indian displays her wares. Travelers may hike in nearby mountains and visit remote islands on the lake, which stretches across a high Andean valley on the Peru-Bolivia border. Credit: Scott Graham through unpopulated countryside and offer tremendous views as they drop to the ocean. In particular, the six-hour ride from San Jose to Limon is world-renowned for its spectacular scenery. If you've a choice, take the ride down to the coast only—the slow climb back to San Jose takes several hours longer. Finally, buses and mini-buses go virtually everywhere there are roads.

Travel and accommodations are relatively inexpensive in Costa Rica, including internal flights, which average $20 to $30 each way, and car rentals, which benefit from the availability of repair parts thanks to the relatively robust Costa Rican economy.

Costa Rica is one of the world's largest coffee exporters. Its affluence (by developing-world standards) is mainly a result of that cash crop. The country also exports bananas grown on plantations on both coasts, and actively courts the importation of hard currency by allowing foreigners to own land. While such a practice is common in industrialized nations, it is unusual in Latin America. The result of this policy, for Costa Rica, has been an influx of North American retirees coming south to buy property and enjoy the country's tropical climate. The retirees' pension checks go a long way in affordable Costa Rica. The situation is good for Costa Rica's finances, too. After convincing a retiree to come south, the country is guaranteed a steady source of valuable hard currency—in the form of the retiree's pension checks—for years to come.

Spanish is the primary language in Costa Rica, but many locals have a working knowledge of English. English is the primary language of the blacks who live on the coasts.

Even if you'll be visiting Costa Rica during the heart of the dry season, be sure to bring rain gear. If you'll not be doing any hiking, an umbrella will suffice. The reason Costa Rica is so lush and green is that even during the dry season, afternoon showers are likely in many parts of the country.

Costa Rica is the only Central American country that has successfully eradicated malaria within its borders. Thus, if you'll be visiting only Costa Rica, you need not take antimalarial pills.

Geography

Geographically, Costa Rica is straightforward. A string of volcanic peaks running roughly northwest to southeast separates the coastal lowlands bordering the Pacific Ocean on the west from the lowlands running to the Caribbean Sea on the east. San Jose, with its 1 million residents, is the largest of several cities that lie in a central valley surrounded by volcanic peaks. Those cities together account for the majority of the country's 2.5 million people. The Caribbean coast is generally wetter and more verdant than the Pacific coast, which is known for its outstanding beaches.

Costa Rica's varied geography accounts for the tremendous range of bird, animal and plant species found within its borders. The small country is home to some 850 bird species, compared to the 650 found in all of Canada and the United States combined. In addition, Costa Ricans share their country with half a million different insects, including a thousand butterfly species. Howler monkeys, jaguars and elusive ocelots roam the lowland jungles, while giant sea turtles land on the beaches to lay their eggs after 20 years at sea. By way of fauna, Costa Rica has more than 1,800 tree species and 1,500 species of orchids.

Climate

Costa Rica has two distinct seasons each year: rainy and dry. Along the Caribbean coast, these seasons are more appropriately described as rainy and not-so-rainy. The dry season runs from December or January to April or May, and is definitely the best time for backcountry travelers to visit.

It rains as much as 300 days a year on the Caribbean coast and the eastern mountainsides, so be prepared for precipitation no matter when you visit the country. Like most foreign visitors, the locals do most of their vacationing in the country during the dry season. Beaches are especially crowded on dry-season weekends and during the Christmas-New Year and Easter holidays.

Since Costa Rica is near the equator, temperatures are determined more by altitude than by season. Winter temperatures are slightly cooler than summer temperatures. However, temperature swings are much more extreme between the lowlands, where they'll hover in the 80s and 90s (30s centigrade), and the highlands. Chirripo, the highest mountain in Costa Rica at 12,533 feet (3,820 meters), is known for its tundra, glacial lakes and subfreezing temperatures. Be aware that hypothermia can be a real risk on the country's highest peaks. Plan your wardrobe and gear list accordingly.

Adventure-Travel Possibilities

Costa Rica is one of the most popular destinations for adventure travelers in all of Latin America. And for good reason. Universal Press Syndicate reporter John Rasmus writes that Costa Rica is "good news for the nature-minded traveler. While Costa Rica's national parks and reserves are fairly rustic, they are nonetheless designed for visitors. That means adequate-to-good hotels near most parks, and a decent system of roads—many of them paved—linking the most-visited attractions. Rental jeeps and four-wheel-drive vehicles are plentiful and reasonably priced in San Jose, the logical starting point on the Pan-American Highway. Guides and maps are easy to come by. And Costa Rica's small size makes it easy to see the entire country in a week or two, even if you're traveling on your own."

By far the best way to visit the backcountry is to visit Costa Rica's national parks. If your time in the country is limited, your only problem will be deciding which parks to see.

In general, the parks can be reached by private vehicle—four-wheel-drive sometimes comes in handy. None of the parks is more than a long day's drive from San Jose. In addition, public buses go directly to many parks and to within walking distance of others. The few roadless parks are reached by boat from the nearest road or by plane from San Jose.

For the latest information on Costa Rica's national parks, visit the National Park Service office in San Jose. The park service will apprise you of the latest conditions at the parks and will provide you with information on how to get to the parks that interest you. The following list of the most popular parks in Costa Rica and their attractions begins with the parks in the northwestern part of the country, then covers those farther south on or near the Pacific coast. The highland parks are covered next, then those on the Caribbean side of the country.

Santa Rosa National Park (1): Santa Rosa was the first national park established in Costa Rica. It is located in the driest area of the country, on the Pacific coast in the northwest, near the Nicaraguan border. Hiking trails wind through the park's rolling, dry savanna to the coast, which is a sanctuary for the Pacific sea turtle. Santa Rosa is well-known to birders, who make use of the many water-hole blinds provided by the park.

Rincon de la Vieja National Park (2): Rincon de la Vieja is an active volcano with nine craters. The two-day climb to its summit, one of the premier backpacking trips in Costa Rica, is best attempted in April or May. Three species of monkeys live on the volcano's slopes, while more than 300 bird species have been identified in the park's 34,000-acre territory.

Barra Honda National Park (3): Located across the Gulf of Nicoya from Puntarenas near the town of Nicoya, Barra Honda is known for its underground caverns and hiking trails. Guides may be hired at the park entrance.

Monte Verde Biological Reserve (4): Monte Verde is a small area of dense forest on the mountainside above the Pacific coast near Puntarenas. The reserve is home to orchids and the rare quetzal, the sacred bird of the Mayan Indians. The reserve was started by a group of Quakers who live nearby and produce delicious cheeses from milk provided by the area's many small dairy farms.

Carara Biological Reserve (5): The reserve is a dense jungle near the Pacific coast south of Puntarenas. Its trails take visitors through thick vegetation alive with multicolored birds, leaf-cutter ants and monkeys. Jaguars, pumas and ocelots live in the park's farthest reaches.

Manuel Antonio National Park (6): This small park offers two of Costa Rica's best features: dense jungles and magnificent beaches. The park is 50 miles (80 kilometers) by air from San Jose. To cover that distance, visitors may choose a 19-minute plane flight or a five-and-a-half-hour drive over mountainous roads. Coral reefs close to shore make for good snorkeling off the park's beaches, while trails snake into the jungle, allowing views of squirrel monkeys, three-toed sloths and toucans. The park is crowded at Christmas and Easter.

Corcovado National Park (7): Corcovado, on the southwestern coast, offers all that Manuel Antonio offers, but on a much grander scale. The 100,000-acre park may be reached by plane from San Jose or by boat from the coastal town of Golfito. The park's coast has two black-volcanic-sand beaches, while its interior contains virgin rainforest. The park is so rich in flora and fauna that 300 bird species, 139 mammal species, 116 amphibian and reptile species, and more than 100 species of trees may be found on one of its acres. Some 90 percent of the visitors to the remote park are scientists working on research projects. Today, the park is threatened by local gold miners using high-impact mining techniques along the park's rivers. Their struggle to make a living at the expense of the park's diverse species of flora and fauna is representative of the struggle between conservation and rapacious land use in much of Latin America.

Braulio Carrillo National Park (8): This sprawling, 80,000-acre park is only 15 miles (25 kilometers) from San Jose. Its facilities are still being developed, but it is a terrific area nonetheless for hiking and birding.

Poas Volcano (9): A good road leads to the top of Poas, making it one of the few easily accessible active volcanos in the world. It is only 25 miles (40 kilometers) north of San Jose, which means it is heavily visited. Visitors should arrive as soon after dawn as possible for good views since clouds often close in early. Guided descents take adventurous hikers a thousand feet into the crater. Other hiking trails allow exploration of more of the park's 10,000 acres. Because the volcano is heavily visited, it is more of an educational park than a wilderness area. Visitors should dress warmly. Although not as high as Irazu or Chirripo, Poas' summit can be quite cold.

Irazu Volcano (10): At 11,260 feet (3,432 meters), Irazu is the highest volcano in Costa Rica. Like Poas, a road leads to the summit of Irazu, which can be reached by public bus from Cartago, the former capital of Costa Rica. More expensive tour buses make the trip from San Jose, 45 miles (70 kilometers) to the west.

Chirripo National Park (11): Chirripo is the highest mountain in Costa Rica at 12,533 feet (3,820 meters). Located in the south-central part of the country, the 100,000-acre park that includes the peak is a wonderland of glacial lakes and tundra. Trails leading to the peak and throughout the park make for ideal hiking and backpacking. December through March is considered the best season to visit Chirripo.

Cahuita National Park (12): This well-developed beach park south of Limon on the Caribbean coast is popular with scuba divers and snorkelers. Cahuita's offshore reef, with its 30 types of coral and 500 species of fish, has been declared a national monument. The good weather of the dry season results in the year's clearest water for snorkelers and divers.

Tortuguero National Park (13): Tortuguero is a tropical island just off Costa Rica's northern Caribbean coast. The island is best known—and named—for the sea turtles that migrate to its beaches each year from April to August to lay their eggs at night in the sand. Tour groups often fly to Tortuguero, but it is easy for independent travelers to take a bus from Limon north to Moin, and a boat from there to the island, where camping and lodging are available. A watch hut has been built on the beach for use by visitors observing the turtles at night.

After visiting a few parks, you'll undoubtedly be ready to enjoy a few of Costa Rica's premier beaches. The best and most accessible beaches are west of San Jose near the port city of **Puntarenas (14)** on the Pacific coast. If you want to avoid crowds, take the ferry from Puntarenas across the gulf to the Nicoya peninsula. Its coastline is dotted with pleasant beaches and tiny villages that can be reached by a combination of roads and walking trails.

The beaches south of the town of Cahuita on the Caribbean, including Cahuita National Park, are the best the Caribbean coast has to offer. Since the Caribbean beaches are found along a fairly short stretch of coastline, they can be quite crowded during dry-season weekends.

Information Sources

The best guide for visitors to Costa Rica is undoubtedly Paul Glassman's *Costa Rica* (Passport Press). From a superb historical overview to detailed information on hotels, restaurants and the country's many national parks, Glassman provides all the information needed by visitors to Costa Rica. In addition, as one review of the book puts it, "the combination of writing style, common sense and wry good humor make this book a pleasure to read."

Visitors who plan to spend time hiking in Costa Rica's national parks would do well to augment Glassman's book with *Backpacking in Mexico and Central America* (Bradt Publications), which provides detailed accounts of hikes and volcano climbs in the country.

Another book worth considering by those planning to visit Costa Rica's national parks is *The National Parks of Costa Rica* (Incafo), by Mario Boza and Rolando Mendoza, available only from bookstores in Costa Rica. The book is not aimed at backcountry travelers, but it does provide extensive descriptions of the parks and their plants and wildlife.

In addition to Glassman's book, another travel guide that covers Costa Rica exclusively is *New Key to Costa Rica* (Publicaciones en Ingles), by Beatrice Blake and Anne Becher. For travelers, the book's main drawback lies in the fact that its authors have tried to make the book many things for many readers. As a result, much of the book is given over to information aimed at retirees and others coming to live in the country. However, the book still contains good advice for visitors, including maps and adequate descriptions of the national parks, popular beaches and other points of interest.

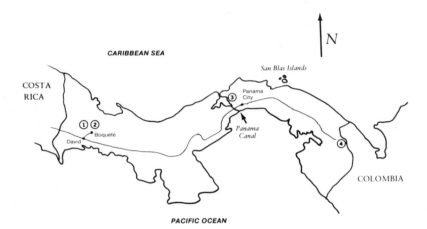

CARIBBEAN SEA

COSTA RICA

San Blas Islands

Panama City

Panama Canal

David

Boquete

PACIFIC OCEAN

COLOMBIA

N

KEY

1) Baru Volcano
2) Third of November Trail
3) Gatun Lake
4) Darien Gap

PANAMA

MILES

0   100

KILOMETERS

0   100

(Map for general location
purposes only)

Chapter 13

Panama

Overview

Ever since the United States engineered the armed insurrection in 1903 that resulted in independence from Colombia for Panama and construction of the Panama Canal for the United States, relations between the two countries have been close. Those relations have been strained in recent years by calls in Panama for sovereignty over the U.S.-controlled Canal Zone and by the 1989 U.S. invasion of Panama to unseat Panama's strongman leader, Manuel Noriega. Still, many North Americans live in Panama, English is widely spoken, and the American dollar continues to be used as the country's adopted currency. For visitors to Panama, that means travel in the country is simple even for those who don't speak Spanish.

For the outdoor enthusiast, a visit to Panama is worth considering for several reasons. There are good hiking and backpacking in the mountainous region around 11,400-foot (3,475-meter) Baru Volcano near the border of Costa Rica in western Panama. Several day and overnight hikes provide bird-watching opportunities near the canal in central Panama. And one of the best-known adventure-travel journeys in all of Latin America—the trek through the swamps and jungles of the Darien Gap separating Central and South America—begins where the Pan-American Highway ends, 60 miles (100 kilometers) east of Panama City. (The Pan-American Highway continues south from Colombia.)

Panama and Guatemala are the only nations in Central America that still have significant numbers of full-blooded indigenous peoples. While Panama doesn't match Guatemala's hundreds of culturally diverse Indian tribes, it does serve as home to the

Guaymi in areas near the Costa Rican border, the Cuna on the San Blas Islands off the north coast and in the jungles of the Darien Gap, and the Choco, who share the Darien Gap with the Cuna.

A few important considerations if you visit Panama:

* Unlike the rest of Central America, travel, food and lodging in Panama are not cheap. Prices are double to triple those of neighboring Costa Rica.

* Theft and robbery are problems in Panama's larger cities, including Panama City, the capital. Keep your possessions under lock and key, stay in better parts of town and don't travel at night.

* You'll need some sort of onward ticket to be allowed into Panama. A return bus ticket from Panama to Costa Rica is adequate.

Geography

Panama is a country of low-lying swamps, rainforests and jungles. It is perfect breeding ground for mosquitoes, some of which are carriers of malaria and yellow fever, the diseases that decimated crews working on the Panama Canal in the early 1900s. Be sure to be vaccinated for yellow fever before traveling to Panama, and bring with you pills to ward off malaria, along with plenty of bug repellent.

Panama straddles the Central American isthmus between Costa Rica and Colombia. The Panama-Colombia border marks the southern terminus of Central America and the beginning of the South American continent.

The geography of Panama is flat except near the Costa Rican border, where a range of mountains rises to an average height of 3,000 feet (900 meters).

Climate

Since Panama lies near the equator, temperatures are hot year-round. The country is extremely wet. As much as 150 inches (380 centimeters) of rain fall each year along the Caribbean coast.

Panama has the same winter dry season as the rest of Central America, only shorter—from January to March.

The Pacific coast of Panama is considerably drier than the Caribbean coast, but it is by no means a desert. The only place in Panama that doesn't share the rest of the country's hot, wet weather is the western highlands. There, instead of being hot and wet, the climate is cool and wet.

Remember, however, that Panama's generally uncomfortable heat and dampness are responsible for the country's verdant, flower-filled jungles and rainforests, and for the wide variety of birds and wildlife found in them.

Adventure-Travel Possibilities

In western Panama, the mountain town of Boquete, above the city of David on the Pan-American Highway, serves as a good base for highland walks. The summit of **Baru Volcano (1)**, the highest point in Panama, is a popular day climb from Boquete. Another hike skirts the northern flanks of Baru from Boquete to the village of Cerro Punta. It may be done as a one-day or overnight hike.

Boquete is also the nearest sizeable town to the start of the rugged *Tres de Noviembre* **(Third of November) Trail (2)**. The trail climbs north to the crest of the Continental Divide, then drops all the way to the Caribbean coast. It is possible to walk the trail in three days. The route is steep and slippery in some places, hard to follow in others, and there are several challenging river crossings en route. Guides for the trek—a virtual necessity—may be hired in Boquete.

Several day hikes and trips—all near **Gatun Lake (3)**—enable visitors to view Panama's abundant bird life along the route of the Panama Canal near Panama City. One follows the deserted, 14-mile-long (33-kilometer-long) road running from the canal-side town of Gamboa through the forest to Gatun Lake. There are several good campsites along the road, or the hike may be done in a day from Panama City by using the scenic railway that runs along the canal to reach Gamboa in the morning and to return to Panama City in the evening.

There is also good day hiking near Gatun Dam at the Gatun stop on the railway. There you'll also see ships being raised and lowered from the level of the Caribbean Sea to lake level by the Gatun locks.

Finally, for $10, you can spend the day at Barro Colorado Island on Gatun Lake. Barro Colorado is a heavily jungled biological reserve teeming with tropical birds and other wildlife. Be forewarned, however: the island also teems with biting insects, including mosquitoes, flies and ticks.

The **Darien Gap (4)** is situated in far eastern Panama. The journey through the Gap involves a combination of walking and catching rides on canoes and riverboats. It is best undertaken in January, just after the rains have ended, when the rivers and streams are still high enough to be navigable. The journey takes from eight to twelve days, depending on your physical condition, your luck in catching boat rides, and the weather.

Some food and rudimentary shelter are available at the Indian encampments you'll pass along the route. Still, you'll need to be self-sufficient, with mosquito netting or tent, hammock or sleeping pad, and a water filter or iodine. And, as at everywhere else in Panama, don't forget to bring bug repellent—lots of it.

Information Sources

Backpacking in Mexico and Central America, by Hilary Bradt and Rob Rachowiecki (Bradt Publications), offers a good overview of Panama, as well as specific descriptions for exploring its backcountry areas. The authors devote a separate chapter to the Darien Gap, in which they provide the most detailed description of the trek available.

Geoff Crowther provides an adequate description of the Darien Gap trek in his book, *South America on a Shoestring* (Lonely Planet Publications).

CARIBBEAN SEA

N

TRINIDAD

Caracas

Orinoco River

GUYANA

COLOMBIA

BRAZIL

KEY

1) Merida
2) Ciudad Bolivar
3) Ciudad Guyana
4) Para Falls
5) Orinoco delta
6) Angel Falls
7) Gran Sabana
8) Avila National Park
9) Morrocoy National
   Marine Park
10) Los Roques Archipelago
   National Park

VENEZUELA

MILES

0   200

KILOMETERS

0   200

(Map for general location
purposes only)

Chapter 14

Venezuela

Overview

For many years, Venezuela served as little more than a stopover for visitors flying from North to South America. Caracas, the capital of Venezuela, was simply a noisy, crowded way station on the journey south to well-known South American backcountry areas like the high Andes of Peru or the wilds of Brazil's Amazon basin. In recent years, however, Venezuela has begun to gain a well deserved reputation as a good destination for adventurous travelers in its own right. To be sure, Caracas is still noisy and crowded. But word is out that a range of backcountry excursions, from mountain hikes to jungle exploration, awaits visitors who venture beyond Venezuela's crowded coastal region.

In South America I met two travelers who had just spent six months exploring Venezuela's backcountry. Both swore adamantly that, to them, Venezuela offered the best backcountry travel opportunities in South America. And neither could say enough about the friendliness and helpfulness of the Venezuelans they had met during their half year in the country. Of course, you needn't spend six months exploring Venezuela's backcountry. Two or three weeks are more than enough for a good visit to the country's best wilderness destinations.

Venezuela is remarkably affordable. A few years ago, Venezuela was one of the most expensive countries in Latin America, but recent economic problems in the country have changed that. Venezuela's enormous international debt coupled with low oil prices worldwide has brought on steep inflation that has made life difficult for many Venezuelans. That inflation has made the country inexpensive for those possessing hard currency.

Venezuela has been one of the world's leading exporters of oil ever since vast amounts of that precious commodity were discovered in northwestern Venezuela in the early 1900s. Despite attempts by the government to encourage other export-oriented industries, oil still accounts for more than 90 percent of Venezuela's total export receipts. The petro-money that has poured into the country since the discovery of oil has paid for the good transportation infrastructure that makes travel around Venezuela fairly easy today. Modern, divided highways carry the country's heavy traffic through Caracas and along the Caribbean coast. Of more interest to those headed for the backcountry, many paved roads stretch inland from the coast. Those roads are traveled by buses and taxis. Rental cars are also available in Caracas.

Geography

Venezuela sits on the northern coast of South America, bordered by Colombia on the west, Brazil on the south and Guyana on the east. Venezuela is not a small country; its 352,000-square-mile (912,000-square-kilometer) land mass makes it larger than France and West Germany combined. Most of Venezuela's population is crowded along the tropical Caribbean coast. Caracas, centrally located on the Caribbean coast, is the largest city in Venezuela, with a population of more than 4 million.

Inland, Venezuela has four major geographic regions. In the far northwest are dry plains of little interest to visitors. It is there that most of the country's oil is extracted. East of the plains is a range of the Andes Mountains stretching into Venezuela from Colombia. That range, the Sierra Nevada de Merida, contains the only snow-covered mountains in the country. In its center, near the mountain city of Merida, is Pico Bolivar, at 16,427 feet (5,007 meters) the highest peak in Venezuela.

East of the Merida mountain range, the Orinoco River flows more than 1,500 miles (2,400 kilometers) across the center of Venezuela. It widens to form a huge, swampy delta before emptying into the Caribbean just south of the islands of Trinidad and Tobago. The Orinoco basin drains more than 80 percent of the water that falls on Venezuela. Much of the basin is covered by virtually impenetrable forest. Attempts are being made to clear and tame the Orinoco basin. In the meantime, the area remains the realm of the jungle Indian and the intrepid explorer.

South of the Orinoco basin, covering all of southeast Venezuela, are the Guyana highlands. The highlands, too, are little inhabited and little explored. They are an area of immense tropical forests, vast, rolling grasslands, and remote flat-topped sandstone peaks called *tepuis*, which rise thousands of feet from the surrounding countryside. The tops of the *tepuis* are often shrouded in clouds and mist. Waterfalls cascade from the *tepuis* to the forests and grasslands below. Canaima National Park, the largest in the country, encompasses a remote area of the highlands known as the *Gran Sabana* (great savanna) in far southeastern Venezuela.

Climate

The Venezuelan climate is hot and tropical, although temperatures cool a little bit in winter. Winter is also the dry season in Venezuela—specifically, from December to April—making it the season preferred by visitors. During those months visitors can count on being rained on less than during the rest of the year, and temperatures in the lowlands—at least at night—will be bearable. Temperatures in the mountains are comfortably cool year-round.

Adventure-Travel Possibilities

The possibilities for outdoor travel in Venezuela center on three of the country's four backcountry areas: the Merida mountain range, the Orinoco basin and the Guyana highlands.

The mountain city of **Merida (1)**, located in the heart of the Venezuelan Andes southwest of Caracas, is the most popular tourist destination in Venezuela. It is also a good base from which to explore the Merida mountain range. From 5,330-foot (1,625-meter) Merida, the world's highest cable car carries passengers more than 10,000 feet (3,000 meters) up to the top of Pico Espejo at 15,629 feet (4,764 meters). The cable car offers a quick way for backpackers to enter the high country. The lack of gradual acclimatization, however, can bring on altitude sickness.

Hiking trails wind throughout the Merida range. Backpackers and day hikers can start out from the semitropical city of Merida at the base of the mountains, from the three cable-car stations en route to Pico Espejo, from Pico Espejo itself, or from road-end Indian villages in the mountains, which may be reached from Merida by bus or taxi. One of the most popular hikes in the Merida mountains is the loop that takes hikers to Pico Espejo and through the Indian villages of Los Nevados and El Morro before returning to the city of Merida.

Pico Bolivar is right next to Pico Espejo, so, if the cable car is running, reaching the highest point in Venezuela is an easy 1,000-foot (305-meter) climb.

The vast Orinoco basin stretching across central Venezuela offers limitless opportunities for those who want to explore jungle terrain. The two largest cities on the Orinoco, **Ciudad Bolivar (2)** and **Ciudad Guyana (3)**, serve as transportation centers for the iron ore mined in the region. They are also good bases from which to visit the Orinoco backcountry.

In earlier times, Ciudad Bolivar was used as a base by Venezuela's most famous son, Simon Bolivar, who led the revolutionary army that liberated the region encompassing present-day Venezuela, Colombia, Ecuador, Peru and Bolivia from Spanish rule in the early 1800s. Bolivar led his army from Venezuela southward across the Andes, engaging the Spaniards in numerous battles along the way. After his early defeats, Bolivar used Ciudad Bolivar, then called Angostura, as a place to rest and regroup.

Today, the pretty colonial city is a good jumping off point for excursions into the Orinoco jungle. Because the Orinoco has been little visited by adventure travelers, you'll be faced with setting up your own backcountry excursions. There simply aren't enough visitors to the Orinoco to support the kind of local adventure travel agencies that exist in other, tourist-oriented jungle towns in South America like Iquitos, Peru, and Manaus, Brazil. Setting up your own journey takes some legwork and the ability to bargain, but the rewards are tremendous.

Most excursions in the Orinoco basin are not easy, and they require dugout canoes. It may take several days to reach a distant destination—days of being cramped in the same tight position in a canoe beneath a relentless sun or a pouring rain, but days also of passing unimaginably beautiful jungle scenery, of brilliant orchids and long, green vines, of screeching monkeys and chattering parrots.

One of the most popular river trips in the Orinoco basin is the three-day journey up the Caura River, a tributary of the Orinoco, to 700-foot (200-meter) **Para Falls (4)**. The return trip down river takes two days. One day is generally spent climbing the steep, 4-mile (7-kilometer) trail up the walls of the Caura gorge to the top of the falls. More days could be spent exploring the clear waters of the Nichare River, a tributary of the Caura. The banks and waters of the Nichare teem with wildlife, including huge freshwater turtles, broad-winged herons and darting kingfishers. The area is the territory of the Maquiritare Indians, whom you may meet along the way in their light dugout canoes. Boats and boatmen for the Caura trip may be hired in Maripa, three hours by road up the Orinoco from Ciudad Bolivar. The best months for the trip are January to March, the heart of the dry season, when fewest bugs will plague you.

From Ciudad Guyana, 60 miles (100 kilometers) downstream from Ciudad Bolivar, head farther downstream to the labyrinthine **Orinoco delta (5)**. The delta is inhabited by Indians who continue to live, work and dress as they have for centuries. Passenger boats ply the river as far downstream as Tucupita, which may also be reached by road. From Tucupita, dugouts may be hired to venture farther into the huge delta.

The highlight of many a traveler's visit to Venezuela is the trip to **Angel Falls (6)**, the highest free-falling waterfall in the world. The fact that the 2,648-foot (807-meter) falls weren't discovered until the 1930s is a perfect example of just how little the Venezuelan backcountry has been explored over the years. Not until Jimmy Angel, an adventurous bush pilot from Missouri, flew over the falls in 1936 did anyone except the few Indians living in the region know that a waterfall 15 times higher than Niagara existed in the world. A year after he first saw the falls, Angel returned with his wife and two friends and landed atop the huge, sandstone *tepui* from which the falls plummet. When their plane sank in the marshy ground where it had come to rest, the four struggled back to civilization after an eleven-day epic overland journey. Angel's plane remained where it had foundered for 33 years until 1970, when it was lifted off the *tepui* by helicopter and transported to Ciudad Bolivar. Today, Angel Falls can be reached in several days by river from Ciudad Bolivar (only possible in the rainy season) or in less than an hour by plane from Caracas, Ciudad Bolivar or Ciudad Guyana.

Two expensive lodges cater to visitors to the falls, or you may choose to camp in the area. Boats to the base of the falls run only during the rainy season. During the dry season, you'll have to be content to view the falls from your plane window as you come in to land.

The looming sandstone *tepui* from which Angel Falls plummet and other *tepuis* in the untracked wilderness area south of Ciudad Bolivar mark the boundary between the jungles of the low-lying Orinoco basin and the Guyana highlands farther south. The **Gran Sabana (7)** encompasses the southernmost part of the highlands. Much of the Sabana is included in the 7-million-acre Canaima

National Park, which includes Angel Falls in its northwest corner and stretches southeast all the way to the Brazilian border. Canaima is larger than all 25 of Venezuela's other national parks combined. The lands protected by the park are a national treasure. The rough dirt road south from Ciudad Guyana through Canaima National Park to the Brazilian border town of Santa Elena passes through areas of lush vegetation and gorgeous scenery, past lakes and rivers, and near numerous soaring tepuis. Hiking, backpacking and camping throughout the park are superb.

Although the coast of Venezuela is densely settled, there are several coastal areas worth exploring.

Avila National Park (8) protects a small range of mountains standing between Caracas and the coast 25 miles away. Despite the fact that the park is literally in Caracas' backyard, it is filled with wildlife and is not too crowded. Trails wind through the park's thick tropical forests and to the top of several peaks, including Pico Occidental, the highest at 8,130 feet (2,478 meters). A cable car runs from Caracas to a ridge near the peak, providing an easy start to hikes in the area. Camping in the park is popular. If you don't have a tent, several huts along the trails are available.

Morrocoy National Marine Park (9), a four-hour drive west from Caracas, was created in 1974 to protect the Morrocoy lagoon, with its mangrove swamps, sea-bird rookeries and coral reefs. Despite a loud outcry when the creation of the park was announced, 1,700 weekend homes then situated on the lagoon were removed and plans for a high-rise hotel and condominium complex complete with golf course were scrapped. Today, the lagoon's sheltered waters and white-sand beaches are reserved for campers and day visitors who enjoying swimming, snorkeling, diving and sailing.

Los Roques Archipelago National Park (10) in the Caribbean north of Caracas provides a quieter, less crowded sun and sea experience than Morrocoy for those who take the trouble to reach the offshore paradise. You must hire a plane or boat to take you to the archipelago, but the effort is worthwhile. Los Roques consists of some 300 islands, 40 of which are large enough to be named. The islands are known for their white-sand beaches, blue lagoons and extensive coral reefs. Diving, snorkeling and just plain relaxing are favorite pastimes on the islands. There is one small fishing village on the archipelago's main island, El Gran Roque, where rudimentary lodging is available.

Information Sources

Because Venezuela is just beginning to be discovered as an adventure-travel destination, there is little literature available to help in planning a visit. The best book on travel in Venezuela is the expensive *Guide to Venezuela,* by Janice Bauman and Leni Young (available through Passport Press). The $30, 925-page book is a truly exhaustive guide to every nook and cranny in the country. The book is aimed at visitors traveling by car, but if you dig deep enough, you'll find that it includes plenty of information on hiking, camping and travel in Venezuela's backcountry.

In its 130 pages, Hilary Bradt's *No Frills Guide to Venezuela* covers the basics on travel in Venezuela plus plenty of information lacking in the *Guide to Venezuela* on backcountry activities in the country.

Geoff Crowther's *South America on a Shoestring* (Lonely Planet Publications) and *Michael's Guide to Ecuador, Colombia and Venezuela,* by Michael Shichor (Inbal Travel Information Ltd., Hunter Publishing, Inc.), offer cursory looks at travel in Venezuela.

Recommendations for bicycling the highways of Venezuela are provided by author J.P. Panet in his book *Latin America on Bicycle* (Passport Press).

The best armchair adventurer's book on backcountry travel in Venezuela is the uproarious *In Trouble Again: A Journey Between the Orinoco and the Amazon,* by Redmond O'Hanlon (Atlantic Monthly Press). O'Hanlon recounts in often gruesome, always hilarious detail the events of his journey into the farthest reaches of the Orinoco basin.

"Venezuela's Islands in Time" is the title of an article in the May 1989 issue of *National Geographic* magazine on *tepuis.* The article provides an excellent overview of Venezuela's unique sandstone towers.

"Venezuela's Andean Hideaway" is the title of an article on Merida—the city *and* the mountains—that appeared in the travel section of the *New York Times* on November 5, 1989.

CARIBBEAN SEA

Barranquilla

Cartagena

N

VENEZUELA

PACIFIC
OCEAN

Bogota

ECUADOR

BRAZIL

PERU

KEY

1) Providencia
2) Los Katios National Park
3) Tayrona National Park
4) El Tuparro National Park
5) Purace National Park
6) San Augustin
   Archaeological Park
7) Isla de Gorgona
   National Park
8) Santa Marta mountain range
9) Sierra Nevada del Cocuy
10) Leticia

COLOMBIA

MILES

0   200

KILOMETERS

0   200

(Map for general location
purposes only)

Chapter 15

Colombia

Overview

Although Colombia is beautiful and varied, it is one of the least visited countries in Latin America. No adventure-travel tours explore its remote mountain ranges. Independent visitors rarely travel by river boat through Colombia's part of the Amazon basin. The many traditional Indian tribes living in Colombia's back-country rarely play host to travelers wandering through the Indians' villages on the network of well-worn trails that stretches throughout the Colombian highlands. Instead, those travelers who do visit Colombia generally stick to well-traveled roads.

Colombia is rarely included on travelers' lists because of pervasive blood-letting by guerrilla revolutionaries, plus the existence of the infamous drug trade in Colombia. Colombia is full of guerrilla revolutionary groups and drug lords with their personal armies. The threat of sudden, unexpected violence between the various factions fighting for power in the country is ever-present in Colombia. While those violent outbursts rarely involve tourists, they occur often enough to convince most travelers to avoid Colombia altogether, or to pass through the country quickly on well-traveled routes to reach other destinations.

Colombia's past is as troubled as its present. Several Spanish conquistadors fought for the right to rule the region in the 1500s. After the country gained independence from Spain in the early 1800s, internal fighting picked up where the conquistadors left off. Two full-scale civil wars have been fought in Colombia during the last hundred years.

Despite the wars, Colombia has been governed since independence by a close-knit ruling class of pure European extraction.

Meanwhile, the vast majority of the population, who are *triquenos* (various mixtures of European, black and Indian blood), has continued since colonial times to live in poverty.

In spite of Colombia's troubled present, travelers do visit the country. During my travels in other parts of South America, I've met several people who have traveled for weeks at a time in Colombia in recent years. None reported any problems; all were impressed by the open welcome they received wherever they went in the country. Indeed, one of the most recently released Lonely Planet Publications books is *Colombia: A Travel Survival Kit*. Obviously, some people are going to Colombia.

Should you decide the attractions of Colombia outweigh the risks involved, you would do well to keep several things in mind:

* Street crime is common throughout Colombia and is rampant in the country's large cities. Police officers are often the worst offenders, although impostors run a close second. Theft is common, outright robbery only slightly less so. Trust no one, carry as little cash as possible, use hotel safes where available, and don't travel at night.

* Avoid the low-altitude regions where coca, the derivative of cocaine, is grown. If you choose to backpack or hike in Colombia, do so in Colombia's highlands.

* If you'll be traveling off the beaten path, come equipped with an official-looking letter of introduction—the fancier the letterhead and the more stamps and signatures, the better. Show it to the suspicious police officers who lurk in many small towns. Avoid the small-town police whenever possible; be respectful and patient with them when you cannot.

Colombia's major cities are easily reached by plane. From there, local and long-distance buses run throughout the country.

Geography
Colombia is a large country of amazing geographic diversity. It is the only country in South America to have coastlines on both the Pacific and Atlantic oceans. It has the highest coastal mountain range in the world. In addition, the Andes Mountains rise from north-central Colombia and stretch southward all the way to the southern tip of the continent. More than 50 percent of the country is lowlands lying east of the Andes.

Its 27 million people make Colombia the third most populous country in South America, just behind Argentina, whose 28 million people are spread out over an area more than twice that of Colombia. (Brazil with its 120 million people is by far the most populated country in South America.) Nearly 90 percent of Colombia's populace lives in the densely settled highlands. Highland villages not connected by road are instead attached one to another by well-used and well-maintained footpaths. Hence, hiking in the highlands is a simple and usually pleasant process of choosing two likely looking villages on a map and setting out to cover the territory between. Wherever there are villages, there will be trails.

Colombia's 440,000-square-mile (1.1-million-square-kilometer) land mass makes it nearly as large as Alaska. On the Caribbean coast, the Santa Marta mountain range rises steeply to a height of more than 19,000 feet (5,790 meters), higher than any other coastal range in the world. At 19,029 feet (5,800 meters), Cristobal Colon peak, named after Christopher Columbus, is the highest point in the Santa Marta range and in Colombia.

South of the compact Santa Marta range, the Andes run north to south as three separate ranges: the Cordillera Occidental in the west, nearest the Pacific coast, the Cordillera Central, and the Cordillera Oriental, which drops off to the lowlands of the Orinoco and Amazon river basins in the east. At 18,865 feet (5,750 meters), Nevado del Huila is the highest peak of the Colombian Andes. It lies in southern Colombia in the Cordillera Central. Except for steamy Barranquilla on the Caribbean coast, all of Colombia's large cities lie in the fertile valleys of the highlands. Bogota, the capital and the largest city in the country with 5 million people, lies in the Cordillera Oriental near the center of the country.

Southeast of the Cordillera Oriental are the virtually uninhabited, nearly impenetrable jungles and rainforests of the Amazonian lowlands. The lowlands cover a third of the country. They reach as far south as the Colombian border town of Leticia on the banks of the Amazon. North of the Amazonian lowlands, Colombia's share of the Orinoco basin is a vast, barren grassland area known as *Los Llanos*.

Climate

Equatorial Colombia's seasons are either dry or wet. Temperatures change little throughout the year. Coastal and interior lowland areas are hot and muggy. Inhabited highland areas range from warm to cool, depending on altitude. Only Colombia's highest mountains are covered by snow and glaciers. Temperatures in the high mountains range from warm on a sunny day to well below freezing at night.

There are two dry seasons in the highlands. The longer and more predictable dry season runs from December to March; there's a shorter, wetter stretch of dry weather in July and August. Los Llanos has only one dry season, from December to March. Rains are likely in the Amazonian lowlands throughout the year. The northernmost part, nearest Los Llanos, is drier from December to March than during the rest of the year. Farther south, in the part of the Amazonian lowlands that includes the tourist town of Leticia, the opposite is true: the wettest months are December to March, and the driest are July to November.

Adventure-Travel Possibilities

One of the most enjoyable and relaxing—although not too adventurous—destinations in Colombia is not on the mainland at all. Rather, it is the Colombian island of **Providencia (1)** north of the Colombian resort island of San Andres in the Caribbean Sea. Visitors may stay at any of several campgrounds on tiny Providencia while enjoying its quiet, pristine beaches and crystalline waters.

Inderena is the government office in charge of Colombia's national parks. There are more than 30 designated national parks in the country, of which only a few are developed. Some of the parks' backcountry areas are used as bases by one or another of Colombia's ten established guerrilla groups. The main *Inderena* office in Bogota can steer you toward those parks that are safe. Note that many of the parks are difficult to reach by public transport. Some of the best are:

Los Katios National Park (2), on the Panamanian border in extreme northwestern Colombia, which is excellent for hikers. Its many trails wind through thick tropical forests filled with birds and butterflies.

Tayrona National Park (3), on the Caribbean coast, with its small, secluded beaches, verdant jungle growth and more than 300 bird species.

El Tuparro National Park (4), the second largest park in Colombia, located on the banks of the Orinoco River. The park protects extensive forests, swamps and grasslands.

Purace National Park (5), a mountain park in southwestern Colombia where hiking, backpacking and climbing are popular.

San Augustin Archaeological Park (6), also in southwestern Colombia, with its extensive tombs and statues.

Isla de Gorgona National Park (7), which protects a tiny, mountainous island of jungles and white-sand beaches just off the Pacific coast.

Other areas for hiking, backpacking and climbing in Colombia include:

The southern slopes of the **Santa Marta range (8)** in northern Colombia, where visitors wander among the highest mountains in the country and through Arhuaco and Kogi Indian villages.

Sierra Nevada del Cocuy (9), a compact range of high mountains near the Venezuelan border in northern Colombia.

Leticia (10), in far southeastern Colombia, the main town from which to visit the Amazonian lowlands of Colombia. There, a thriving tourist trade exists, taking visitors on tours of the jungle during the July-to-November dry season. Leticia is reached by plane from Bogota. Other areas of the Amazonian lowlands in Colombia are generally considered off limits because of extensive cocaine production and trafficking throughout the region.

Information Sources:

Lonely Planet Publications' *Colombia: A Travel Survival Kit*, by Krzysztof Dydynski, does an excellent job of directing visitors toward Colombia's backcountry. Dydynski describes in detail many visits to national parks and other mountain and rural walking areas.

You may wish to augment Dydynski's book with *Backpacking in Venezuela, Colombia and Ecuador*, by Hilary and George Bradt (Bradt Publications), if you can find it. Although out of date, the book provides good descriptions of hikes in the Colombian backcountry.

Finally, *Michael's Guide to Ecuador, Colombia and Venezuela*, by Michael Shichor (Inbal Travel Information Ltd., Hunter Publishing, Inc.) provides a good overview of Colombia for travelers passing quickly through the country.

PACIFIC
OCEAN

COLOMBIA

N

①(600 miles or
1,000 kilometers to
the west)

⑪

⑨

⑧ Quito

② Rio Napo

⑦

Misahualli

Banos

⑥

⑩

②

⑤

Guayaquil

③

④ Cuenca

PERU

KEY

1) Galapagos Islands
2) Oriente
3) Trail from Guasuntos
   to Ingapirca
4) Las Cajas National
   Recreation Area
5) Sangay National Park
6) Chimborazo
7) Cotopaxi
8) Pichincha
9) Otavalo
10) Tungurahua
11) Atacames

ECUADOR

MILES
0   100

KILOMETERS
0   100

(Map for general location
purposes only)

Chapter 16

Ecuador

Overview

B isected by the equator, the small republic of Ecuador straddles the South American Andes, from the warm Pacific coast on the west to the steamy jungles of the Amazonian lowlands to the east. Between are Ecuador's mountains—lower, gentler versions of the rugged Andes farther south in Peru, Bolivia, Chile and Argentina. Jutting up from the Ecuadorian Andes, glacier-clad volcanoes hover at close to the 20,000-foot (6,000-meter) level on both sides of Ecuador's green, fertile central valley. The highest is 20,702-foot (6,310-meter) Chimborazo. It and several other volcanoes offer straightforward, accessible ascents for beginning high-altitude climbers. Tougher routes on those volcanoes and routes on more remote volcanoes provide plenty of challenge for more experienced climbers. The Galapagos Islands lie 600 miles (1,000 kilometers) west of the Ecuadorian coast. There, animals never hunted by man cavort unafraid near human visitors.

The majority of Ecuadorians are of mixed Indian-European descent. However, indigenous Indian populations survive, primarily descendants of Incan and pre-Incan civilizations who live in the highlands. The best known highland Indians are the Otavalenos. The 35,000 Otavalo Indians live in a region of the Andes north of Quito. They are known primarily as weavers; the rugs, belts, sweaters and bags they produce are prized around the world. Each Saturday in the town of Otavalo the Indians display their wares in a market that covers three plazas and spills into adjoining streets. Tourists and Otavalenos barter side by side for the goods produced on looms that are fixtures of every Otavaleno home. As a result of their weaving prowess, the Otavalenos are one of Latin America's most prosperous indigenous peoples.

Ecuador is one of Latin America's more prosperous countries, thanks to the discovery of oil in Ecuador's Amazonian lowlands in the 1970s. In addition, Ecuador's moist climate makes farming a fairly successful occupation in much of the country. Ecuador is certainly better off economically than its fellow Andean republics to the south, Peru and Bolivia.

Travel within the country is fast and convenient in buses plying Ecuador's many paved highways (often at breakneck speeds). Cars and jeeps may be rented for prices comparable to those in North America. Internal flights are heavily subsidized by the government. As a result, except for flying to the Galapagos, the most expensive internal flight in Ecuador is less than $20. At more than $300 each way for foreigners (as compared to $40 for Ecuadorians), the cost of flying to the Galapagos is truly exorbitant—the Ecuadorian government knows a cash cow when it sees one. Still, for those who can afford it, the price is worth paying, since the islands are certainly one of the world's most fascinating nature reserves.

Geography

Although Ecuador is little larger than Great Britain, it is a land of incredibly varied geography. Mountains and jungles, beaches and rolling hills, lowland rainforests and treeless, highland plains known as *paramo* all lie remarkably close together. This mixture makes Ecuador a perfect destination for travelers wishing to explore a variety of backcountry landscapes in little time.

Most tours of Ecuador begin in Quito, which sits at 9,000 feet (2,750 meters) above sea level in the heart of the central valley. After La Paz, the capital of Bolivia, Quito is the second highest national capital in the world, yet since it lies only a few miles south of the equator, Quito's 1 million residents enjoy comfortable, shirt-sleeve weather year-round.

In 1802, Alexander von Humboldt, a German scientist studying Ecuador's volcanoes, dubbed the central valley, studded on both sides by glacier-covered volcanoes, as the "Avenue of the Volcanoes." The name is used to this day, and with good reason. On clear days, 18,996-foot (5,790 meter) Cayambe is visible north of Quito and 19,347-foot (5,897-meter) Cotopaxi is visible to the south. Also south of Quito lie Chimborazo, El Altar, the twin Iliniza peaks,

Antisana and, farthest south and most remote, the perpetually mist- and storm-shrouded Sangay.

The fertile central valley, with its abundant rainfall, is Ecuador's breadbasket. Nearly half the country's 8 million inhabitants live in the valley and adjoining highlands. The other half live in the coastal lowlands to the west, where most of Ecuador's cash crops, like bananas and coffee, are produced.

Ecuador's slice of the Amazonian lowlands east of the Avenue of the Volcanoes is known as the Oriente. Today only a few thousand people call the Oriente home, but that is changing quickly as more and more oil is discovered in the region. For now, roads to the Oriente are of rough dirt. When they're not washed out by landslides, a trip down them from the highlands winds through deep, green gorges spouting a waterfall from every crenelation. The Oriente itself is a flat region of thick rainforest. It is cut by brown, sluggish rivers flowing to the Amazon from the highlands to the west. The rivers are the only "highways" in the Oriente. Dugout canoes laden with people and supplies ply the rivers throughout the year. Most of those who live in the Oriente make their homes either in squalid oil towns hacked out of the jungle or near the banks of the various Oriente rivers. Out their back doors is true Amazonian rainforest, penetrated only by indigenous Indians of the area and by increasing numbers of adventure-travel agencies offering travelers the opportunity to tramp and boat through undeveloped parts of the Oriente for anywhere from a day to two weeks.

Climate

Rob Rachowiecki notes in his book, *Climbing and Hiking in Ecuador*: "Most descriptions of Ecuador's climate agree that its most reliable aspect is its unreliability." Still, some generalizations are possible, the first of which is that Ecuador is wet. Even during the dry season in Quito, rain is a common occurrence. In the Oriente, the dry season barely has a chance to begin before the wet season sets in again. No matter when you visit Ecuador, bring rain gear.

The absence of winter, spring, summer and fall as we know them in North America is more apparent in Ecuador than in other tropical countries because Ecuador sits smack on the equator. As a result, mean temperatures barely change throughout the year, and you can count on 12 hours of daylight and 12 of darkness no matter when you arrive.

The wet and dry seasons—unreliable though they are—determine the best times to visit. In general, the dry season on the coast is from July to November. Although it rains throughout the year in the Oriente, the least wet months are September through December. Remember that it is always hot in the Oriente and along the coast because of their low altitude. The best months to visit the Galapagos, whose climate is controlled by the cool Humboldt current, are May to September. The highland dry season runs from June to September, and a short spell of dry weather usually occurs around Christmas.

As for the volcanoes, each creates its own micro-climate, which depends mostly on that particular volcano's proximity to the humid Oriente to the east. The wettest, stormiest months on volcanoes near the Oriente—like Cayambe, Antisana, El Altar and Sangay—are June to August, and the driest months are December and January. On the western side of the Avenue of the Volcanoes, little more than 50 miles (80 kilometers) from the eastern side, the situation is the opposite. The driest months for climbing and hiking in the mountains on the western side of the central valley are June to September. However, there is a short length of dry weather around Christmas, coinciding with the eastern side's dry season.

Adventure-Travel Possibilities

In recent years, Ecuador has become one of the most popular adventure-travel destinations in Latin America. As a result, visitors can travel in Ecuador by a wide variety of means.

Independent travel by rental car or local bus in the country is convenient and easy to arrange, and lodging is comfortable and affordable. English is widely spoken, although independent travelers would do well to arrive with a rudimentary grasp of Spanish.

For those wishing to visit Ecuador as part of an organized tour, the possibilities are nearly endless. Adventure-travel agencies based in North America and in Ecuador offer a variety of packages in a range of prices.

The **Galapagos Islands (1)** are Ecuador's premier destination for travelers looking for a unique, remote environment in which to spend a week or two. The islands were made a national park in 1959. Today they are host to tens of thousands of visitors a year. Those visitors are subject to strict, conservationist regulations. As a result, the flora and fauna of the islands have remained generally well-protected even as the number of visitors to the islands has grown.

The Galapagos are home to flora and fauna that have evolved over hundreds of thousands of years isolated from the South American mainland. The Galapagos flora and fauna were important in the development of Charles Darwin's theory of evolution after his visit in 1835. Today, plants and wildlife that have been largely undisturbed by man greet all Galapagos visitors. Trails that wind through the barren, lava-rock islands enable visitors to view plants, birds, sea lions, penguins and iguanas. Perhaps the best way to experience the Galapagos is by snorkeling in the islands' countless bays. There, floating on the surface of the water or swimming about just below, visitors commonly come face to face with giant, curious sea lions, flitting penguins, huge sea turtles and graceful sea rays.

There are only two ways to visit the islands: with an all-inclusive tour from the mainland, or by flying to the islands independently and setting up your own tour from there. Setting up your own tour is less expensive but more problematic. It may take a day or two to organize a group of independent travelers and to find a captain with a boat willing to follow the group's itinerary at an agreeable price. The advantage is that you'll be a member of an independent group subject to its own itinerary rather than that of a tour agency.

The **Oriente (2)** is another popular destination for adventure travelers. Adventure-travel agencies in both North America and Ecuador offer a range of tours to Ecuador's Amazonian lowlands that vary in comfort, arduousness and price. It's also easy to arrange independent travel in the Oriente.

Most tours of the Oriente begin at the Rio Napo, a large tributary of the Amazon east of Quito, and move on to more remote areas of the rainforest. In recent years, the town of Misahaulli has developed into a small but thriving tourist center serving those looking for affordable trips into the jungle. Travelers have only to show up in town. This is easily done by bus from Quito, assuming the spectacular road down from the Andes isn't washed out. Once in Misahaulli, tours may be arranged with other travelers that generally range in duration from a day to two weeks. Average price is $10 to $20 per day, including meals.

Organized tours originating in Quito are the most popular way to visit the Oriente. For $50 to $100 a day you'll be flown to one of the small airstrips in the Oriente, met there by vehicle and transferred to dugout canoes that will take you to a comfortable jungle lodge. From the lodge, you'll be able to explore the surrounding rainforest as you choose. An example of a typical Oriente lodge is *La Selva* ("the jungle"), located 60 miles (100 kilometers) down the Rio Napo from the oil town of Coca. From the lodge, guests can choose excursions into the rainforest that fit their idea of adventure, from guided walks on marked trails to strenuous overnight hikes that make visitors feel, as one participant put it, "like the real Indiana Jones."

River trips can also be undertaken in the Oriente. One popular, easy-to-arrange trip is the six-hour run from Misahualli down the Rio Napo to Coca, from which buses and regular plane flights return to Quito. A large passenger-dugout makes the run every other day for a few dollars per person. Personal dugouts may be hired by groups of up to ten to make the run for about $90. The stretch along the river from Misahualli to Coca is populated—huts dot the river bank every few miles. Aside from the colorful birds of the rainforest, wildlife is rarely seen. Still, the trip offers a taste of the beauty of the rainforest for those whose time is limited. Conversely, the truly adventurous may set off down the Rio Napo from Misahaulli or Coca and emerge at the mouth of the Amazon weeks later, having traveled on a variety of passenger and cargo vessels along the way.

Exploration of Ecuador's Andean highlands is done in two ways: hiking and backpacking in the region, and mountain climbing.

Hikers and backpackers can explore a range of areas. Sections of the stone-paved Inca road system that stretched for thousands of miles through the Andes at the height of the Incan empire 500 years ago still exist in the backcountry of southern Ecuador. The most popular stretch of remaining Inca road leads hikers from **Guasuntos to Ingapirca (3)**. The route traverses a 14,000-foot (4,250-meter) pass and winds through remote rural areas where Andean Indians follow ways of life little changed through the centuries. After two or three days of hiking, the trail ends at Ingapirca, the largest and best-preserved Inca ruin in Ecuador.

The colonial city of Cuenca is 30 miles (50 kilometers) south of Ingapirca. Twenty miles (30 kilometers) west of Cuenca is **Las Cajas National Recreation Area (4)**, an enchanting area of treeless, highland grassland known as *paramo*. No trails are maintained in the park. Instead, visitors are free to roam from one to another of the preserve's countless lakes, camping where they like. Occasionally, the rare Andean condor is spotted in the area.

A demanding backpacking trip in the remote **Sangay National Park (5)** traverses the eastern range of the Ecuadorian Andes near the misty Sangay volcano and drops into the rainforests of the southern Oriente. The trip takes at least a week and requires route-finding abilities.

The areas of *paramo* surrounding the two highest mountains in Ecuador, **Chimborazo (6)** on the western side of the Avenue of the Volcanoes and **Cotopaxi (7)** on the east, provide excellent back-packing possibilities. Cotopaxi National Park, which encompasses Cotopaxi volcano and a large expanse of surrounding *paramo*, is the most developed of Ecuador's national parks. One popular backpacking trip in the park is the week-long circuit around the peak on a combination of little-traveled dirt roads and hiking trails, and across open country. Other backpacking possibilities in the area include the trails leading to deep, walled valleys at the base of 15,000-foot (4,575-meter) Ruminahui, and to other lesser peaks on the fringes of the park. A challenging three- to four-day hike goes cross-country for 30 miles (50 kilometers) from Cotopaxi to the glacier-topped Antisana volcano.

From Quito itself, a popular acclimatization day hike heads out of the city and up the flanks of **Pichincha (8)**, an extinct volcano looming over the city to the west.

North of Quito, many trails take day hikers into the verdant hills surrounding the town of **Otavalo (9)** that are home to the Otavaleno Indians.

In recent years, Ecuador has become popular with beginning and intermediate high-altitude mountain climbers. As gear improvements have opened the sport of high-altitude climbing to more enthusiasts, word has spread that Ecuador's volcanoes offer many good beginner's routes. In as little as two weeks, budding climbers can acclimatize and attempt two or three ascents.

Climbers' huts stand at the base of the most popular routes up the volcanoes, making the climbs simple propositions. Since the permanent snow level near the equator (15,000 feet or 4,575 meters) is the level of most of the huts, climbs of Ecuador's volcanoes can be done in one long day with only a light summit pack.

The only negatives about climbing in Ecuador are the relatively warm temperatures and the intense sun, which make the snow on the peaks soft and avalanche-prone by mid-morning. Hence climbs in Ecuador begin between midnight and 3 a.m, after a few hours of sleep. Note too that temperatures on the peaks are only relatively warm. Anything above 19,000 feet (5,790 meters), especially before sunrise, is quite cold. Climbers must dress accordingly to avoid frostbite. Plastic boots may be rented in Quito along with other essential equipment: crampons, ice axes and ropes.

Cotopaxi is the second highest peak in Ecuador at 19,347 feet (5,897 meters). More attempts are made on its summit than any other peak in Ecuador because the route to the top is direct, not too steep and generally free of hidden crevasses. The climber's hut on Cotopaxi is only an hour by car from Quito.

The highest peak in Ecuador, 20,702-foot (6,310-meter) Chimborazo, is the second-most-attempted peak in the country. The standard route on Chimborazo is fairly safe, with little crevasse danger and only two short, steep pitches that occasionally require the placement of protection.

The tenth-highest peak in Ecuador, 16,457-foot (5,016-meter) **Tungurahua (10)**, is popular with non-technical climbers. Only crampons and an ice axe are necessary for negotiating the snowfields near the summit of the peak. After reaching the top, climbers may descend to the nearby tourist town of Banos, there to soak away the pains of the climb in the town's hot springs.

After you've had enough of the mountains, the beaches of Ecuador's Pacific coast offer the opportunity to play in the sun and surf. The small, relaxed resort town of **Atacames (11)** on the northern coast is the most popular destination on the coast.

Information Sources

Rob Rachowiecki's *Climbing and Hiking in Ecuador* (Bradt Publications) is an excellent guide to exploring Ecuador's Andean highlands and to climbing its peaks. Rachowiecki covers every highland hike and climb mentioned here in adequate detail and he includes fascinating historical and informational tidbits. The author also offers information on exploring the Oriente and the western lowlands.

Rachowiecki is also the author of Lonely Planet's *Ecuador and the Galapagos Islands: A Travel Survival Kit* (Lonely Planet Publications). In his conversational, straightforward style, Rachowiecki provides as much information on travel in Ecuador as any independent traveler could possibly need. In addition, Rachowiecki is an informed conservationist who offers good advice on protecting Ecuador's cultural and natural resources.

Another helpful, but not essential, book for travelers planning to visit Ecuador's backcountry is *Backpacking in Venezuela, Colombia and Ecuador,* by Hilary and George Bradt (Bradt Publications), which is hard to obtain. The book details hikes in 12 regions of Ecuador and provides humorous, helpful anecdotes as well.

Michael's Guide to Ecuador, Colombia and Venezuela (Inbal Travel Information Ltd., Hunter Publishing, Inc.), by Michael Shichor, provides a concise, well-written description of what to see and do in Ecuador, with detailed advice for visiting the Oriente and the Galapagos, and short descriptions of climbing Cotopaxi and Chimborazo.

Two books are aimed at guiding travelers through the problematic process of selecting and embarking on tours of the Galapago Islands. Both provide natural-history information on the islands as well. They are *The Galapagos Islands* (The Mountaineers) and *A Traveller's Guide to the Galapagos Islands* (Bradt Publications).

The book known as the birdwatcher Bible for visitors to the Oriente is *A Guide to the Birds of Colombia* (Princeton University Press), by Steven Hilty and William L. Brown.

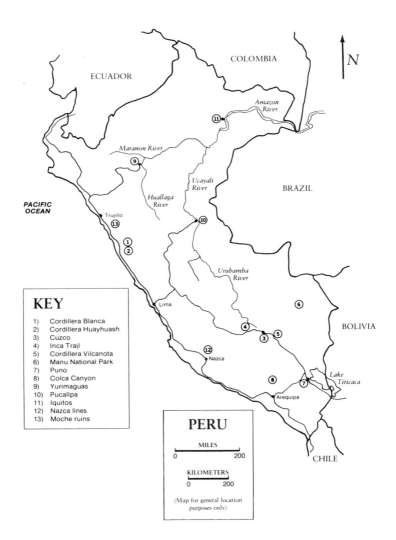

COLOMBIA

ECUADOR

Amazon River

⑪

Maranon River

⑨

Ucayali River

PACIFIC
OCEAN

Trujillo
⑬

Huallaga River

BRAZIL

①
②

⑩

Urubamba River

Lima

⑥

BOLIVIA

KEY

1) Cordillera Blanca
2) Cordillera Huayhuash
3) Cuzco
4) Inca Trail
5) Cordillera Vilcanota
6) Manu National Park
7) Puno
8) Colca Canyon
9) Yurimaguas
10) Pucallpa
11) Iquitos
12) Nazca lines
13) Moche ruins

④

③ ⑤

⑫
Nazca

⑧

Lake Titicaca

⑦

Arequipa

PERU

MILES

0   200

KILOMETERS

0   200

(Map for general location
purposes only)

CHILE

N

Chapter 17

Peru

Overview

For years, Peru has been one of the most popular adventure-travel destinations in Latin America. Today, despite political and economic problems that threaten the stability of the country's government, Peru remains a popular destination for adventure travelers. The northern Peruvian Andes offer some of the most remote hiking possible in Latin America on trails that wind among some of the most impressive mountains in the world. The country's southern Andes contain the mysterious Incan ruins of Machu Picchu. The Inca Trail leading to Machu Picchu is the most popular trek in Latin America. On average, 6,000 visitors walk the trail each year. In addition to good hiking, Peru's *cordilleras*, or mountain ranges, provide some of the most challenging technical climbing in the world. The Cordillera Blanca alone, for example, has 22,205-foot (6,768-meter) Huascaran and 19 other peaks over 20,000 feet (6,000 meters). Beyond the mountains to the east, the Amazonian frontier towns of Yurimaguas, Pucallpa and Iquitos serve as jumping off points for a range of jungle travel opportunities. Along Peru's desert coast lie the mysterious Nazca lines and the intriguing ruins of the pre-Incan Moche civilization. In the dry coastal mountains of southern Peru is the deepest gash in the earth, the Colca Canyon, which drops 14,339 feet (4,370 meters) from its rim on one side and 10,607 feet (3,233 meters) on the other. That's more than twice as deep as the Grand Canyon. For the stout of heart and limb, hiking trails wind all the way to the bottom of the Colca.

Cuzco, the former capital of the Incan empire, is in Peru as well. The empire stretched throughout the Andes when the conquistadors arrived from Spain in the 1500s. In the preceding hundred years, the empire had expanded rapidly from its base in the Cuzco area by conquering neighboring tribes and installing a system of rigid governmental control. A common language was instituted— Quechua, which remains the primary language of many Peruvian Indians today. The Incan religion, which involved sacrifices and festivals in honor of the sun god and *pachamama*, or mother earth, was instituted as well.

The Incas used some of the wealth accumulated from their conquered subjects to build an extensive road system. When the conquistadors arrived, stone-paved Inca roads snaked throughout the Andes, to the Amazonian lowlands and to the Pacific coast. The roads stretched from what today is Ecuador to central Argentina and Chile.

Cuzco fell to the conquistadors soon after their arrival early in the 16th century, and the last mountain strongholds of the Incan rulers fell within the next few years. The empire collapsed quickly for several reasons. For one, the arrival of the conquistadors coincided with the climax of a bitter and bloody feud between two brothers fighting for control of the empire. That feud plus the recent, rapid expansion of the empire had left the Incas susceptible to attack. In addition, the Spaniards' horses and metal armor made them largely invulnerable to the Incas' weapons.

Thus were a handful of Spanish invaders with a few hired warriors able to bring about the collapse of one of the most advanced civilizations the world had known to that time. Within a few years of the empire's collapse, the Spaniards had melted down the Incas' gold and shipped it home, where it financed Spain's ongoing wars with its European neighbors. In the New World, the port city of Lima replaced Cuzco as the capital of the region, Catholicism was introduced to replace the Incan religion and Spanish was introduced to supersede Quechua.

In recent times, the ruins of the Incas' temples and palaces in and around Cuzco have become a great tourist draw. For the backcountry enthusiast, remaining sections of the Inca road system provide hiking routes near Cuzco and throughout the Andes.

Today, Peru is deeply in debt, inflation is surging out of control, and guerrilla groups—primarily the Maoist *Sendero Luminoso*, or Shining Path—have sprung up in the mountains. The Peruvian government has worked to protect the popular tourist areas around Huaraz in the north and Cuzco and Machu Picchu in the south. Adventure-travel tours still explore the backcountry of both regions. Because the situation is fluid, however, be sure to check the latest before setting off. As it stands now, it is best to travel in Peru's backcountry only with a group, either by signing up for a tour or by joining other independent travelers.

As in other Latin American countries, thievery has long been a problem in Peru for Peruvians and foreigners alike. Keep your passport, return plane ticket and money in a passport holder or money belt beneath your clothes, and keep a close eye on the rest of your gear at all times.

Geography

Peru sits on the Pacific coast of South America. Its territory encompasses the middle of the longest continuous mountain range in the world—the Andes. The mountains account for 25 percent of Peru's area, while the Amazonian lowlands east of the continental divide account for 60 percent. The remaining 15 percent is coastal desert running the length of the country. Peru is situated between the neighboring Andean republics of Ecuador to the north and Bolivia to the south. With a total area of half-a-million square miles (1.3 million square kilometers), it is nearly twice as big as Texas.

The chief means of transportation used by visitors to Peru are bus and air. Long-distance buses of varying quality go virtually everywhere in Peru. By North American standards, they are extremely inexpensive. Roads in the Peruvian Andes are often rough; bus trips through the mountains are arduous and uncomfortable. Instead, many visitors fly to their ultimate destinations in Peru. Visitors who want to explore the Incan culture of the southern Andes generally fly from Lima to Cuzco, and continue overland to Machu Picchu or into the backcountry. Those who want to explore the Amazonian lowlands fly from Lima to any of several jumping-off points on the Amazon basin side of the Andes.

Because of its proximity to the coast, the Andean hiking and trekking center of Huaraz is fairly accessible by bus, as is the white-walled colonial city of Arequipa, the jumping-off point for visits to Colca Canyon. Arequipa is also accessible by air.

Climate

Since Peru is just south of the equator, average temperatures in the country barely change from season to season. The Peruvian winter—from May to September—is the dry season, and hence is best for backcountry excursions.

It never rains on Peru's coastal desert. (Crops grown in the region are irrigated with runoff from the mountains.) Despite the lack of rain, a thick, almost viscous fog covers the coastal region during the dry season. You won't see the sun when you fly into Lima at the start of a dry-season visit to the country, but you won't be rained on either.

Temperatures are hot along the coast, hot and muggy in the Amazon lowlands (where rain is likely throughout the year) and comfortably cool in Huaraz and Cuzco, both of which are higher than 10,000 feet (3,000 meters) in elevation. Only on high-altitude hikes and climbs will you need anything more than a sweater or a light jacket for warmth.

Adventure-Travel Possibilities

Peru is popular with adventure travelers because of the wide variety of backcountry trips available in the country. The three most popular adventure-travel tours in Peru—backpacking in the northern Andes, exploring the Amazon jungle and hiking the Inca Trail to Machu Picchu—may be completed during a three-week visit to the country.

Flying to Peru is affordable—$300 round-trip fares from Miami to Lima are not uncommon. Many airlines fly to Lima from Europe as well. Flights in Peru average $50 to a $100 each way. Since the cost of living in Peru is extremely inexpensive by North American standards—a decent hotel room is $5 to $10 a night, restaurant meals are a dollar or two—a two- or three-week trip by an independent traveler will cost little more than $1,000, including airfare.

The small mountain town of Huaraz has been a popular jumping-off point for backpacking trips into the **Cordillera Blanca (1)**, whose glacier-crowned peaks rise majestically above town in the east. Many hotels and restaurants in town are geared to the tourist trade. In addition, agencies in town offer guided treks in the mountains and climbs of the cordillera's highest peaks. Everything you'll need to undertake a trip or climb in the cordillera is available in Huaraz. Trekking food and stove fuel are easy to find, and several stores rent backpacking and climbing equipment.

The most popular hike in the Cordillera Blanca is known, logically enough, as the Cordillera Blanca Trek. The five-day trek is a loop just south of Huaraz that crosses and then recrosses the spine of the cordillera over two 15,500-foot (4,725-meter) passes. For its entire length, the route winds among heavily glaciated peaks over 20,000 feet (6,000 meters) in elevation, including Huascaran and the soaring white summit pyramid of Alpamayo.

Numerous other backpacking routes snake through the Cordillera Blanca, much of which is preserved by the Peruvian government as a national park. The latest route information is available at the national-park office in Huaraz, where visitors must register and pay a small fee before entering the backcountry.

Technical climbing is a popular activity in the Cordillera Blanca. Huascaran is the most popular climb in the range because of its distinction as the highest peak in Peru. The three- to four-day climb up the normal route is of intermediate difficulty. More difficult routes may be climbed on the mountain, while other peaks in the cordillera offer a range of possibilities to climbers, from rocky scrambles to highly technical rock and ice climbs.

The **Cordillera Huayhuash (2)** is a compact, 20-mile-long (30-kilometer-long) range of high, rugged peaks just south of the Cordillera Blanca. The range contains the second-highest peak in Peru, 21,760-foot (6,632-meter) Yerupaja, and reportedly the most beautiful mountain-and-lake scenery in the country. Unfortunately, the Huayhuash's many hiking trails and climbing routes were effectively off limits to visitors for much of the 1980s because of guerrilla activity in the area.

The Andes surrounding **Cuzco (3)** in southern Peru offer a variety of hiking and backpacking possibilities. A good warm-up is the 5-mile (8-kilometer) day hike that winds through the Incan ruins of Sacsayhuaman, Qenco and Salumpuncu in the hills above Cuzco. Other day hikes near Cuzco take in the sites of the Sacred Valley, home to Incan temples, towns and fortresses in various stages of ruin. All are fascinating to visit, especially by foot rather than by tour bus. The **Inca Trail (4)** is a three- to five-day hike over three 12,000-foot (3,650-meter) passes along an ancient, paved section of Inca road to the magical city of Machu Picchu, the Lost City of the Incas. The route begins west of Cuzco at kilometer 88 on the Cuzco-Machu Picchu railway. The trail passes through several overgrown Incan ruins, and offers views of the surrounding Cordillera Vilcabamba.

Because the Inca Trail is popular with foreigners carrying expensive camping gear, it is popular with thieves as well. Keep all your gear inside your tent at night, even if it means a lumpy night's sleep, and travel only in large groups. Solo hikers and small groups of two or three backpackers have been held up on the trail in the past, although this activity has been curtailed in recent years by beefed-up police and ranger patrols along the route.

There are many other hiking trails in the Vilcabamba, including several variations to the traditional Inca Trail route that add a day or two to the hike to Machu Picchu.

The **Cordillera Vilcanota (5)** lies just east of Cuzco. It is topped by the 20,946-foot (6,384-meter) Auzangate massif and three other peaks close to or above 20,000 feet (6,000 meters) in height. Footpaths used by local Indians wind throughout the high, treeless area below the peaks. Backpacking along the Vilcanota's many trails is popular, as is climbing the range's high peaks.

Rafting trips on the Urubamba River ranging from one to several days are offered by several tour agencies in Cuzco. The Urubamba flows from Cuzco past Machu Picchu and on into the Amazonian lowlands. One- to two-week camping tours deep in the lowland jungles of **Manu National Park (6)** east of Cuzco are offered as well. Manu is the largest national park in Peru. Because it is so remote, it is one of the best places in Latin America to see a wide variety of jungle wildlife. Trips to Manu involve the use of various combinations of chartered light aircraft, train, four-wheel-drive vehicle and dugout canoe to reach and tour the park.

A day's train ride south of Cuzco is the town of **Puno (7)** on the shores of Lake Titicaca. From Puno, boats may be hired to visit the Uros Indians at their villages built atop floating reed islands on the lake. Farther out in the lake are the islands of Taquile and Amantani, which may also be visited by hired boat. The people of these islands are known for their simple, relaxed way of life. Visitors with sleeping bags may spend a night or two on the islands.

The colonial city of Arequipa in southern Peru is the jumping-off point for journeys to remote **Colca Canyon (8)**. Tour agencies in Arequipa offer day trips to the rim of the canyon. Backpackers may take buses to the rim or to small towns in the dry, barren canyon itself, and from there set off on any number of trails that wind down to the Colca River at its bottom. The Colca River offers some of the most challenging whitewater rafting in Peru. It was first run in 1981. Today, a few adventure-travel tours run the river when it is lowest, at the end of the dry season in August.

In addition to Cuzco, three other cities serve as starting points for exploring Peru's Amazonian lowlands: Yurimaguas, Pucallpa and Iquitos. All three are easily reached by scheduled flights from Lima.

The quiet northern town of **Yurimaguas (9)** serves chiefly as a port from which to catch combination passenger-cargo boats down the Huallaga and Maranon rivers to Iquitos on the Amazon River, three to five days away. Boats generally make the journey only about once a week, with no set schedule, so be prepared to spend some time relaxing in Yurimaguas before setting off down river.

The larger city of **Pucallpa (10)** is also a port from which boats can be taken down the Ucayali River to Iquitos, five or six days away. In addition, the affordable lodges on the banks of Yarinacocha Lake, 7 miles (11 kilometers) east of Pucallpa, offer a good base from which to explore the surrounding jungle. Boats may be hired to explore the undeveloped parts of the lakeshore, including the Shipibo Indian village of San Francisco at the lake's northwest end. The Shipibo society is matriarchal, and Shipibo women are makers of fine ceramics and weavers of textiles featuring striking geometric patterns. Their handicrafts may be purchased in San Francisco.

It is easier to find boats to Iquitos from Pucallpa than from Yurimaguas. Boats leave Pucallpa for Iquitos almost daily, although fewer boats are able to make the trip when the Ucayali is low toward the end of the dry season in July and August.

Iquitos (11) is the major jungle city of Peru. With its 200,000 residents, it is the largest city in the Amazon basin that cannot be reached by road. Iquitos is the center of a thriving jungle tourist trade. Tour agencies in the city offer a choice of jungle trips. The basic jungle experience involves a stay of from one to several nights in a jungle lodge located up a remote side stream from the busy Amazon River. Visitors are ferried to the lodges from Iquitos by boat. Meals of typical jungle food are served, and day trips take visitors on wildlife-viewing excursions deeper in the jungle. Those interested in a rougher jungle experience can sign up for group overland trips that involve building sleeping platforms each night or sleeping in remote Indian villages, and hunting and fishing for food. Stays in the jungle lodges near Iquitos run as high as $100 a day, while the overland journeys generally cost about $30 a day.

From Iquitos, visitors can head farther down the Amazon. Leticia, Colombia, located where the borders of Peru, Colombia and Brazil meet, is two to three days away. From Leticia, passenger and cargo boats ply the Amazon all the way to its mouth on the Atlantic Ocean.

Although the Peruvian coast doesn't offer much in the way of adventure travel, a visit to the **Nazca lines (12)** south of Lima and to the **ruins of the Moche civilization (13)** north of Lima are worth including in your itinerary if time permits. The mysterious Nazca lines, made famous by the widely publicized supposition that they were made by extraterrestrials, stretch straight across the desert for miles. They are best viewed from the air by light plane. Ruins of the Moche civilization are found around the northern coastal city of Trujillo. Studies of the ruins have revealed that the Moche civilization, which preceded the Incan empire by more than a thousand years, was in some ways more advanced than the Incan civilization.

Information Sources

If you plan to visit the backcountry around Huaraz, the book *Classic Walks of the World* (The Oxford Illustrated Press), edited by Walt Unsworth, provides a detailed description of the Cordillera Blanca Trek and of a walk in the Cordillera Huayhuash.

Hilary Bradt's *Backpacking and Trekking in Peru and Bolivia* (Bradt Publications) offers accounts of the Cordillera Blanca Trek and several other hikes in the Cordillera Blanca. Bradt also offers detailed descriptions of the Inca Trail to Machu Picchu, day hikes near Cuzco, backpacking trips in the cordilleras Vilcabamba and Vilcanota near Cuzco, climbs of volcanoes near Arequipa, and hikes in Colca Canyon. Bradt's book is packed with useful information by a writer who obviously loves the areas she describes. It is a worthwhile purchase.

Rob Rachowiecki's *Peru: A Travel Survival Kit* (Lonely Planet Publications) is one of the best of the Lonely Planet book series on independent travel in the developing world. Rachowiecki writes with insight and clarity sometimes lacking in other Lonely Planet guides. The author is a devoted backcountry enthusiast who provides plenty of information on the adventure-travel possibilities mentioned earlier in this chapter.

Michael's Guide to Bolivia and Peru (Inbal Travel Information Ltd., Hunter Publishing, Inc.), by Michael Shichor, provides adequate information for visitors who won't be exploring Peru's backcountry. Shichor offers cultural insights throughout the book, including a good thumbnail sketch of the Incan civilization. For those who would like to read a more detailed account of the history of the Incas, John Hemming's *Conquest of the Incas* (Harcourt Brace Jovanovich) is the most detailed available.

If you're considering a visit to Colca Canyon, you might want to track down the November 1988 issue of *Backpacker* magazine. On page 58 is "Peru's Colca Canyon: Where Dry is a Way of Life," *Backpacker* editor John Harlin's account of his rugged trek into a little explored area of the Colca with a group of travel agents and trekking guides.

"The unfathomable ages displayed in the rock somehow seem a little more comprehensible here because of the lack of life," Harlin writes of the barren Colca. "Back home in Pennsylvania, or almost anywhere in America, the overwhelming presence of growing, living things keeps you focused on lifespans that have something in common with your own. Here, on your way down into the Colca, there is no confusion."

If you can find it, *South America: River Trips,* by George Bradt (Bradt Publications), offers two worthwhile accounts on river travel in Peru. One chronicles a journey in several stages by cargo and passenger boat down the Amazon River from Pucallpa, Peru, to Manaus, Brazil. The other is a description of a river trip through Manu National Park in southeastern Peru.

If you're considering signing up for an adventure-travel tour in Peru—or anywhere else in Latin America for that matter—you may wish to take a look at the June/July 1989 issue of *Modern Maturity* magazine. In the article "At Last: City in the Sky" on page 48, writer John Barnard describes in vivid detail his two-week group trek on the Inca Trail to Machu Picchu organized by Wilderness Travel of Berkeley, California. In addition to providing an enjoyable account of trekking the Inca Trail, Barnard offers a perceptive description of what makes group adventure-travel tours the fastest-growing segment of the tourist industry today.

"Wonderful how a random group of people—men, women, young, old—can come together as friends after only a few days of shared adventure and a little common hardship," Barnard notes in his journal. "After no showers, chuckwagon food, bleeding blisters, altitude nausea. After worrying—and then discovering there was really nothing to worry about. The Peruvian Andes? No problem!"

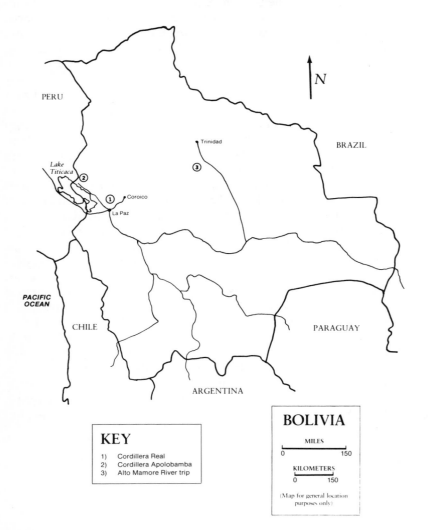

PERU

BRAZIL

N

Trinidad

③

Lake
Titicaca

②

① Coroico

La Paz

PACIFIC
OCEAN

CHILE

PARAGUAY

ARGENTINA

KEY

1) Cordillera Real
2) Cordillera Apolobamba
3) Alto Mamore River trip

BOLIVIA

MILES

0   150

KILOMETERS

0   150

(Map for general location
purposes only)

Chapter 18

Bolivia

Overview

Forget warm beaches, coral reefs, sea kayaking and snorkeling. Instead, picture the most rugged mountains you've ever seen. The Canadian Rockies? The Alps? The High Sierra? Multiply that thought tenfold, and you'll have the rugged Cordillera Real of the Bolivian Andes. Landlocked Bolivia hasn't anything to offer the ocean lover, but mountain maniacs and those drawn to all things rugged consider it a vacation paradise.

Life is hard for many Bolivians. Little rain falls in the *altiplano*, or high plain, where the majority of Bolivia's predominantly Indian population lives. The altiplano is a wide, flat, dry valley between towering ranges of the Andes. Its inhabitants, the altiplano Indians, break and plant their fields by hand during the planting season, and sift through the rock-laden soil at harvest time for the small potatoes that sustain them. Their llama herds roam throughout the region, eating the sparse brown grass that grows beneath the steady equatorial sun. Many times each year, the Indians hold celebrations that are a joyful mixture of Catholicism and the Incan rituals of their forefathers. Costumed in brightly colored tin outfits resembling wedding cakes, their sweating heads supporting giant hats of papier-mache serpents and dragons, they dance and sing while musicians play the haunting, delicate music of the Andes on multi-chambered, reed instruments called *zamponas*.

In Bolivia, visitors learn what enjoying life—with all its problems and harshness—is all about. That alone is worth the price of airfare to Bolivia. In addition to experiencing the stoic, celebratory way of life of the Bolivian Indians, visitors may undertake travel as adventurous as any in Latin America. You may simply travel along the rugged dirt roads of the Bolivian backcountry by the only means of transport often available: huge, bumpy trucks carrying cargo and a top layer of passengers. Or you may strap on a backpack loaded with as much food as you can carry and set off to traverse the Cordillera Real from the altiplano deep into the lush, verdant Amazon basin to the east. Or you may undertake a climb of one of the countless peaks of the Bolivian Andes.

Fully 75 percent of Bolivia's population is full-blooded Indian, while only 5 percent is of pure European extraction. That disparity is the highest in Latin America. Only half of Bolivia's Indians speak Spanish; the rest speak only the languages of their ancestors— primarily Quechua and Aymara.

Bolivia's Indians are survivors of centuries of oppression and exploitation. Hundreds of thousands died as virtual slaves in mines producing tin, silver and gold for the country's Spanish rulers and later for multinational corporations. Even the distinctive bowler hats worn by Bolivian women were imposed on them by one of their Spanish rulers.

Until a few years ago, Bolivians lived beneath the oppressive weight of a failing economy and regularly toppling governments. As recently as the early 1980s, Bolivia's economy, decimated by the collapse of world tin prices, was in shambles. The country was slipping ever deeper into debt, inflation was rampant, spirits were low. Today, things are different. A series of strict, government-imposed austerity measures has stymied inflation, and the economy has stabilized. The industrialized world's appetite for cocaine, much of which is quietly grown and produced in Bolivia, continues to aid the economy as well.

In an effort to lessen its foreign-debt burden, Bolivia has become a leader in negotiating debt-for-nature swaps. Such a swap involves the purchase by an international conservation organization of a small part of the country's debt. In return, Bolivia sets aside a tract of backcountry and agrees to maintain the area as wilderness—still open to some traditional human uses like rubber tapping or farming—under the management of the conservation organization.

Today in the capital, La Paz, and throughout the country, prices for all goods are high as a result of the government-imposed austerity measures. But prices are stable. Gone too, at least for now, are the continual coups and changes of government that were commonplace in Bolivia over the last few decades. In their place has been relative stability marked by open, democratic elections.

As might be expected of one of the poorest nations in Latin America, Bolivia's transportation system is little developed. Trains travel some routes between cities, and a few main roads are intermittently paved. Otherwise, travel in Bolivia is confined to rugged dirt roads. Buses ply many of the roads, but seats are always in high demand, and the aisles are generally filled with paying passengers as well. Large cargo trucks usually add a top layer of paying passengers to their load, and small trucks—usually four-wheel-drive Toyota pickups—travel many routes packed with passengers and their many blanket-wrapped bundles.

Although Bolivia is a rugged, largely undeveloped country, it is still entirely possible to visit comfortably—even while undertaking activities in the backcountry.

There are many good hotels in La Paz, the base for most backcountry journeys in Bolivia. Four-wheel-drive vehicles may be rented in La Paz, albeit for higher prices than in North America and Europe. And private four-wheel-drive vehicles may be hired in the city by backpackers and climbers wishing to be driven to a trailhead or the base of a mountain without delay.

Geography

Most visitors to Bolivia fly into La Paz, which has good air connections with North America. Those coming from sea level often spend a couple of days moving slowly and gasping for breath. At nearly 12,000 feet (3,650 meters) above sea level, La Paz is the highest national capital in the world. In addition, the city is built in a huge bowl-like valley. Thus, most streets in La Paz lead up or, equally, down. Steeply. Indeed, La Paz is the only city I've ever visited whose municipal cemetery features a specially built, four-wheel-drive Jeep hearse to negotiate the steep, cobbled streets around town.

Walking the streets of La Paz is good preparation for what's to come. Most everything of interest to the adventure traveler is higher than La Paz, including Lake Titicaca at the northern end of the Bolivian altiplano. Above the lake to the east tower the peaks of the Cordillera Real, which combines with the Cordillera Oriental farther to the south to seal off the arid altiplano from the Amazonian lowlands beyond. To the west, the lower Cordillera Occidental separates the altiplano from Chile's Atacama Desert, which extends to the Pacific coast.

Bolivia's Amazonian lowlands account for 70 percent of the country's area, yet the region is sparsely populated. Efforts to encourage the Indians of the Bolivian highlands to relocate to the fertile—but humid, rainy and bug-infested—lowlands have proved largely futile. In addition to being stoic, the descendants of the Incas are stubborn.

The altiplano extends from Lake Titicaca and La Paz in the north to the mining regions around Potosi in the south. The altiplano accounts for only 10 percent of Bolivia's area, yet is home to 65 percent of the country's people. Bolivia is primarily rural—only a third of the people live in cities. Although La Paz is growing rapidly, it has yet to turn into one of the mega-cities that have been created in other Latin American countries by dissatisfied *campesinos* flocking to urban centers in search of better lives.

Even La Paz—the largest city in Bolivia, with 1 million residents—is hard to characterize as a city. With Indian salespeople lining the sidewalks, displaying everything from coca leaves to light bulbs, La Paz has more the feel of a large village than of a capital city.

Climate

The altiplano is nearly desertlike in its dryness. The area receives less than 20 inches (50 centimeters) of rain each year. Clouds often billow up and over the mountains from the Amazonian lowlands to the east, but never once in months of travel in Bolivia did I see them cover the dry, brown soil of the altiplano and deliver a soaking rain. Because the altiplano averages more than 12,000 feet (3,650 meters) in elevation, it is cold as well as dry. Average temperatures in the region hover near 50 degrees (10 degrees centigrade).

On the eastern side of the mountains, the situation is reversed. The humid, fertile Yungas region, only 60 miles (100 kilometers) east of La Paz, receives more than 50 inches (125 centimeters) of rain each year. The average temperature in the region is a steamy 80 degrees (27 degrees centigrade). Deeper into Bolivia's Amazonian lowlands, more rain falls and temperatures are even hotter.

Since Bolivia is near the equator, temperatures are fairly constant year round, although the altiplano and La Paz are noticeably cooler during the winter months of June and July. The entire country's rainy season occurs during the summer months of December to April, though the rainy season starts earlier and lasts later in the lowlands than in the altiplano. Indeed, rain is likely year-round in the lowlands.

The backpacking and climbing season in the mountains is mid-May to mid-November. Those who will be hiking into the Yungas may wish to time their visit for the middle of that season, when the lowlands are driest.

Adventure-Travel Possibilities

The Andes are Bolivia's chief adventure-travel draw, especially the rugged **Cordillera Real (1)** east of La Paz. Stone-paved roads laid by the Incas more than 500 years ago still snake through the mountains, over high passes and down deep valleys, providing excellent backcountry trails for modern backpackers. Several mountains in the cordillera close to and above 20,000 feet (6,000 meters) offer beginning and intermediate mountain climbers safe routes on which to practice high-altitude climbing techniques. Only an hour outside La Paz is the world's highest commercial ski area, Chacaltaya, which tops out at over 17,000 feet (5,180 meters). Nearby, at the base of the Zongo glacier, are ice caves that may be visited as part of a day hike in the area.

Many agencies in La Paz offer day tours that include hiking to the ice caves and skiing at Chacaltaya when the area is open—usually from December to mid-May. Chacaltaya is operated by the Bolivian Mountain Club, whose members maintain an office in La Paz and offer their own day tours to the area. Well-used ski equipment can be rented at the area for about $8. The area is essentially a large, triangular snowfield. A quarter-inch steel cable runs up the middle of the slope on pulleys made of old truck wheels. To ascend, skiers hook bent steel bars onto the cable and hang on for as long as they can. This is especially difficult for unacclimatized visitors. In fact, when I skied at Chacaltaya, I found going up more tiring than skiing down! The snow starts out hard early in the day, but becomes mush by noon. Obviously, conditions are far from ideal. But who can pass up the opportunity to ski at 17,000 feet? A day at Chacaltaya is also good acclimatization for those who will be going even higher in the Bolivian Andes.

The Cordillera Real has become a climbers' mecca in recent years for several reasons. First, the sun shines steadily throughout much of the Bolivian winter (which handily corresponds with the summer-vacation season in the northern hemisphere). Second, since Bolivia has been largely ignored by the climbing community in the past, first ascents of many difficult routes are still possible. Third, while bureaucracy makes climbing in the Himalaya increasingly problematic, and as political problems haunt Peru, Bolivia's challenging climbs remain easily accessible.

The most popular mountain in the Cordillera Real for beginning and intermediate climbers is Huayna Potosi, whose height of just over 20,000 feet (6,000 meters) makes it a worthy achievement. Two-wheel-drive taxis can reach the 16,000-foot (4,875-meter) base of the normal route, which is only an hour-and-a-half drive northeast of La Paz. Many beginning climbers attempt the peak each year.

Although the sun shines on the mountains through most of the Bolivian winter, high-altitude climbs in Bolivia require plastic boots (or leather boots with overboots), warm clothing, a warm sleeping bag and a four-season tent. Glacier glasses and sunscreen are essential as well. Unlike in Peru and Ecuador, little gear is available for hire in Bolivia. You'll need to bring everything you need with you, including crampons, ice axe and rope.

Another popular beginning climb in the Cordillera Real is Cerro Mururata, a two-hour drive south of La Paz. Although Mururata is just under the magical 20,000-foot (6,000-meter) elevation, the route to the top is gentle, making it a good warm-up and learning peak.

At 21,201 feet (6,462 meters), Nevado Illimani is perhaps the single most frequently attempted peak in Bolivia. The peak is popular for two reasons. It stands alone just south of La Paz, towering impressively over the city, and it sports a fairly direct walk-up route to the top. Still, the climb takes four days, and the mountain is often raked by high winds. It is not for the inexperienced.

The prime backpacking routes in Bolivia wind through the Cordillera Real. Many routes traverse the range from the altiplano and drop far down into the verdant Yungas region of the Amazonian lowlands.

The Takesi Trail is the most popular backpacking trip in Bolivia. The two- to three-day hike follows the route of an ancient Inca road for 30 miles (50 kilometers). The road is still paved with stones for nearly half its length, and at times is as wide as a two-lane highway. Since the Takesi is well used by visitors and locals, the trail is in great shape even where paving no longer exists. The route crosses a 16,000-foot (4,875-meter) pass, offering tremendous views of Illimani, Mururata and other peaks of the Cordillera Real. All along the route are opportunities to marvel at the incredible engineering feats and craftmanship of the Incan road builders. Since the route ends at the 6,000-foot (1,800-meter) level, the bugs and thick jungle overgrowth found lower in the Amazon basin are not a problem. The route ends on a major road only three hours from La Paz by bus or truck.

Another popular backpacking trip begins at La Cumbre, the pass traversed by the main road from La Paz to the Yungas. From there the route drops steadily for two days to the relaxing tourist town of Coroico at 6,500 feet (1,980 meters), where hotels with swimming pools, sunny balconies and panoramic views of the green Yungas side of the Cordillera Real await.

Another popular two-day route heads north from La Cumbre. It emerges on the road leading to the base of Huayna Potosi. Walked from north to south, the hike may be lengthened to include the descent from La Cumbre to the town of Coroico.

A high, remote route starts at the town of Sorata, which sits at the base of the towering Illampu-Ancohuma massif at the northern end of the Cordillera Real. From Sorata, it is possible to circle the massif via the village of Ancohuma and the Cooco basin, reemerging on the altiplano six to eight days later.

Finally, the remote **Cordillera Apolobamba (2)**, which sits on the Bolivia-Peru border northeast of Lake Titicaca, offers the intrepid explorer weeks of hiking on a good network of high mountain trails constructed by the Incas centuries ago.

In the lowlands, many of the hundreds of rivers that drain Bolivia's share of the Amazon lowlands could conceivably be traveled. However, the area is remote, undeveloped and little explored. Only the **stretch of the Alto Mamore River between Puerto Villaroel and Trinidad (3)** is traveled with any regularity by visitors. Puerto Villaroel is six hours by bus into the lowlands from Cochabamba. From there, it is five days downstream to Trinidad—if you're lucky enough to find a cargo boat going that direction that will allow you to tag along. From Trinidad you can fly to La Paz or make your way back via Santa Cruz by bus and train.

If all this discussion of backcountry travel and mountain climbing in Bolivia sounds like a bit much to you, take heart. Traveling around the country by public transport is adventurous enough—and is certainly rewarding. Many roads in Bolivia cross high mountain passes and offer tremendous views of snowcapped peaks with either the brown altiplano or the green jungle below. In particular, the road from La Paz over La Cumbre and down past Coroico deep into the Yungas has been called by many the most spectacular road in all of Latin America. For much of its length, the road is only one lane wide, which makes for hair-raising views as your vehicle edges out toward the cliff to allow another vehicle to squeeze by. At one point, the road actually goes under a waterfall that drops from hundreds of feet above.

Other routes are nearly as spectacular. In 1988, the *New York Times* printed an article by one of its editors, Edwin McDowell, who chronicled his overland crossing of the Bolivian Andes from La Paz to Cochabamba by bus.

"Crossing the Andes by land is vastly more rewarding than gazing down at the mountains from a plane," McDowell wrote. "The inevitable mechanical breakdowns, the vagaries of climate, the occasional hunger pangs and assorted other vexations pale alongside the opportunity to cross the longest continuous mountain range in the world at ground level—if that term can properly be applied to roads more than two miles high."

Later in his narrative, McDowell noted, "After emerging from one particularly long curve, we found ourselves halfway up a high mountain staring at wave after wave of soaring peaks, some of them turbaned with glistening snow. For the next four or five hours the journey was everything travelers with sturdy hearts could ask for. Magnificent vistas greeted each bend in the road, and in this no less beautiful America, purple mountain majesties unfolded again and again."

Information Sources

The best guide for backpackers and hikers is *Backpacking and Trekking in Peru and Bolivia*, by Hilary Bradt (Bradt Publications). Bradt provides a good cultural overview of the Andean way of life, and offers proven preparatory tips as well. She describes several hikes in the Cordillera Real, as well as a trip in the Cordillera Apolobamba.

Another Bradt Publications book, *South America: River Trips*, offers an account of the trip down the Alto Mamore from Puerto Villaroel to Trinidad.

Bolivia: A Travel Survival Kit (Lonely Planet Publications) provides an excellent overview of Bolivia with plenty of information on overland travel in the country.

The best source of information for climbers is *La Cordillera Real de los Andes—Bolivia* (Editorial Los Amigos del Libro), available only in Spanish and only in La Paz, at the *Libros del Amigos* bookstore on Calle Mercado. The book provides a geographic and climbing history of the Cordillera Real, plus approach and climbing descriptions.

Michael's Guide to Bolivia and Peru (Inbal Travel Information Ltd., Hunter Publishing, Inc.) by Michael Shichor, offers practical information as well as perceptive cultural insights on modern Bolivia.

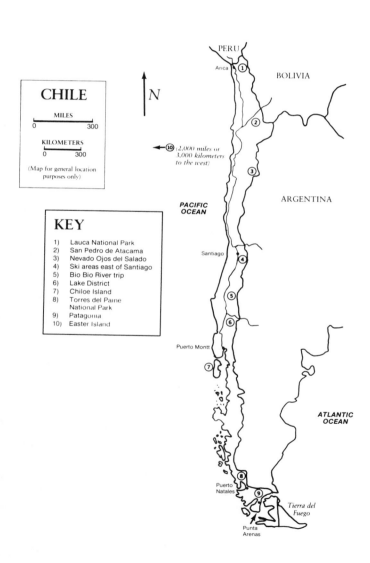

CHILE

MILES

0   300

KILOMETERS

0   300

(Map for general location
purposes only)

N

⑩ (2,000 miles or
3,000 kilometers
to the west)

KEY

1) Lauca National Park
2) San Pedro de Atacama
3) Nevado Ojos del Salado
4) Ski areas east of Santiago
5) Bio Bio River trip
6) Lake District
7) Chiloe Island
8) Torres del Paine
     National Park
9) Patagonia
10) Easter Island

PERU

Arica ①

BOLIVIA

②

③

PACIFIC
OCEAN

ARGENTINA

Santiago ④

⑤

⑥

Puerto Montt

⑦

ATLANTIC
OCEAN

Puerto
Natales ⑧

⑨

Tierra del
Fuego

Punta
Arenas

Chapter 19

Chile

Overview

Chile presents adventure travelers with a variety of backcountry opportunities. Climbers will find in Chile a nearly limitless array of mountains, from the sedate slopes of Osorno Volcano to the extremely technical, vertical rock faces of the Torres del Paine. For non-climbers, the mountains are a largely uninhabited paradise for camping, backpacking and skiing.

Chile stretches for nearly 3,000 miles (5,000 kilometers) along the southern Pacific coast of South America. It is the longest country in South America, but its average width is less than 150 miles (240 kilometers). The Andes Mountains run in an unending string down the eastern border of the country. Most of Chile's 12 million people, the majority of whom are of mixed Spanish-Indian blood, live in Chile's fertile central region.

Visitors to Chile are often pleasantly surprised by how different the country is from most other Latin American countries. Chile boasts a well-developed infrastructure and a populace that is among the best educated in Latin America. A clean, modern subway carries commuters around Santiago, the capital of Chile. High-quality, well-maintained paved roads allow transport to most areas of the country. Private vehicles are a common sight on the roads. Indeed, hitchhiking is easier in Chile than anywhere else on the continent, with the possible exception of Argentina. For those who want their own vehicle, car rentals are simple to arrange in most Chilean cities. Buses also ply Chile's roads, enabling visitors to travel around the country quickly and affordably. Bicycle tourists also appreciate the country's good road system. In the rugged fjord and glacier lands of the far south, boats take over where roads leave off. In addition, LAN-Chile and Ladeco, Chile's national airlines, have flights to cities and towns from one end of the country to the other.

While there is certainly something to be said for experiencing the rough-and-tumble travel of less developed countries like Bolivia and Peru, there is also a lot to be said for the ease and comfort with which visitors can get around Chile. Indeed, for that reason alone, Chile would make an excellent choice for anyone venturing to the developing world for the first time. Combine that ease of travel with Chile's many possible backcountry excursions, and Chile becomes almost unbeatable. The only blemish on such a rosy characterization is the questionable political and economic situation in Chile.

Like most Latin American countries, Chile's history is one of wars and repressive governments. Until the arrival of the conquistadors in the 1500s, Chile was inhabited in the north by Indians ruled by the Incan Empire, and in the south by the Mapuche Indians. The conquistadors conquered the northern Indians, then used them as slave laborers.

After gaining independence in the early 1800s, Chile fought and conquered the Mapuche Indians, who had remained autonomous in the south under Spanish rule. In the late 1800s, Chile won the mineral-rich Atacama Desert in the north in the War of the Pacific with Peru and Bolivia.

Chile expanded economically through the early and mid-1900s. From 1973, when a CIA-sponsored coup overthrew popular leftist Chilean President Salvador Allende, through the 1980s, Chile was ruled by a ruthless right-wing military junta that crushed all dissent through intimidation, imprisonment, torture and outright murder. Meanwhile, the country fell on economic hard times caused primarily by the failure of investments made by the government to industrialize the country and by falling prices on the world market for copper, Chile's chief export.

Those economic problems plus continued political dissent forced the government in the late 1980s to begin opening the door, ever so slightly, to more democratic processes. For the first time since Allende was overthrown, national democratic elections were held in late 1989. No one knows what the ultimate outcome of the elections will be. Meanwhile, two points should be considered by potential visitors to Chile. First, violence in the country has always been confined to those involved in the conflict—dissenters and government forces. Tourists have never been targeted the way they have been at times in other countries around the world. Second, regardless of one's feelings about the Chilean government, the Chilean people are just as welcoming and warm-hearted today as they were before the military came to power in 1973. They enjoy hosting visitors. All the dealings I have had with Chileans during the time I've spent in Chile have been cordial.

Most visits to Chile begin in Santiago, the capital and largest city in Chile with a population of more than 4 million. Santiago is connected by air to North America and to all other South American capitals. Although Chile is not as inexpensive as most Latin American countries, travel in the country—including the cost of domestic flights—is still affordable. Flights to Santiago from North America are more expensive than to most other South American destinations because of Santiago's location far south on the continent. Still, round-trip flights between North America and Chile are available for well under $1,000. Beyond that initial cost, a two- or three-week visit to the country will likely cost independent travelers less than $500, assuming they shun five-star hotels in favor of Chile's many fine mid-range hotels. Those who travel by rental car rather than by public transport can expect to spend somewhat more.

While thievery does exist in Chile, it is not nearly as severe as in other Latin American countries, like Peru and Colombia. Also, because Chile is far enough south of the equator to have a temperate climate, many of the health problems that plague visitors to tropical Latin countries are not a concern in Chile. Diseases like malaria and yellow fever do not exist in Chile, nor are intestinal upsets caused by tropical bugs a major problem.

Geography

The long, spaghetti-thin shape of Chile is truly one of the oddest in the world. Along with its odd shape, the Andes Mountains running the length of Chile's eastern border with Argentina are the country's other constant. Here and there the Andes and the lowlands to the west are studded with volcanoes, many of which are high enough to be covered with snow and glaciers throughout the year. The highest is Nevado Ojos del Salado, on the border with Argentina, which tops out at 22,572 feet (6,880 meters).

North to south, Chile is divided into three distinct geographic zones, each covering roughly a third of the country. The northern third is the barren Atacama Desert, which continues up the coast of Peru and into Ecuador. It is in the Chilean portion of the Atacama that most of the country's mining takes place—for copper, iron, gold and silver. The desert is broken by long oasis-like valleys whose floors are kept perpetually green by snowmelt flowing from the mountains to the sea. Virtually all human habitation of the Atacama is in these valleys. Other than the oasis valleys, the desert is brown and virtually lifeless. The Andes east of the desert are mostly barren below the perpetual snowline as well. Aside from those fed by runoff water, the only plants that survive in the Atacama are a few high-altitude cacti that pull moisture from fog that periodically settles against the western slopes of the Andes.

The fertile central third of Chile differs dramatically from the desert country to the north. Rain falls and plants grow. The population density attests to the quality of life in the area: more than 80 percent of Chile's population lives in the country's fertile central region. East of Santiago, above the agricultural lowlands, are Chile's world-famous ski resorts. Here, skiers from north of the equator find fresh snow during the northern hemisphere's summer. South of Santiago along the Argentinian border is the Lake District. Here, tall mountains and the perfect cones of volcanoes rise far above the perpetual snowline among huge reflecting lakes and lush, flower-filled valleys. The Lake District is laced by backpacking trails and backcountry roads. Many of the lakes in the area are served by small ferries that transport tourists and local villagers, most of whom are of German ancestry. With its Alp-like towns and awe-inspiring scenery, the Lake District is a wonderland for backcountry wanderers.

The southern third of Chile, which begins at Puerto Montt, is as wet and cool as the northern third is dry and sunny. The southern coast of Chile is broken by deep fjords comparable to those that slice deep into the coast of Norway. Chile's fjords have rendered construction of a highway to the south difficult, but a new stretch of highway is pushing south from Puerto Montt. Traditionally, boats have been the logical form of transport along the coast and to the many coastal islands. Chile's southern mountains are bedecked by thick evergreen forests and colorful, spongy tundra. Southern Chile's rugged, natural beauty is not unlike Alaska's far to the north. Only a couple of towns of any significance exist in southern Chile. Both serve as tourist outposts during the area's short summers, when the sun shines for as long as 20 hours a day.

Climate

Chile's climates are primarily temperate. Chile and Argentina are the only countries in South America far enough from the equator to have seasonal climatic changes like those of North America. Chile's seasons are of course directly opposite those of the northern hemisphere. For those planning to visit the backcountry, then, the best months to come to Chile are during the summer, from November to March. Skiers should visit during Chile's winter, from June to September.

Even though the Atacama Desert lies north of the Tropic of Capricorn and thus is officially part of the tropics, it still has Chile's temperate climate. Temperatures in the Atacama don't change much from summer to winter—a tropical trait—but they are almost temperate in their coolness. Average temperatures in the Atacama, which are stabilized by the desert's proximity to the Pacific Ocean, range between 70 and 80 degrees (20 to 30 degrees centigrade) throughout the year. Temperatures don't change that much in the fertile central region of Chile either. Temperatures in the central region rarely drop below freezing during the winter months; snow falls only in the mountains. Only in the far south are seasonal differences great. Winters are long, cold, windy and dark in the rugged south. Snow is heavy in the mountains; rain is common on the coast. Summers are better, but only by a little; rain and cold temperatures are still possible, winds often are fierce. However, the south's tremendous scenery more than compensates for the harsh weather of the area.

Adventure-Travel Possibilities

Chile truly is a paradise for campers and backpackers. The country has made a concerted effort to provide public campgrounds in its many backcountry areas. Those campgrounds are used by Chilean vacationers and foreigners alike. The country has an extensive national-park system, and it has taken admirable steps to protect some of the endangered species of South American animals still surviving within its borders, like the Patagonian puma and the vicuna, a member of the llama family hunted close to extinction for its rich, tender meat.

Two areas are of particular interest to travelers looking to leave the beaten path in northern Chile. A hundred miles (160 kilometers) east of the seaside resort city of Arica in far northern Chile is **Lauca National Park (1)**. Lauca protects an arrestingly beautiful region of high desert country just off the road that runs from Arica to La Paz, Bolivia. The jewel of the park, most of which is over 13,000 feet (4,000 meters), is Lake Chungara, guarded by the snow-capped peaks of twin volcanoes nearby. Lauca is known primarily for the large herds of endangered vicuna it protects. Many bird species live in the park as well, including the rare Andean condor and vast numbers of waterfowl.

Day tours to the park from Arica are common. It is also easy to take an Arica-to-La Paz bus as far as Lauca for several days of backpacking along the park's extensive trail system. Visitors should bring plenty of warm clothing, even for a day trip. No matter how warm and sunny it is in Arica, it will be cold at the park.

The intriguing area around the oasis town of **San Pedro de Atacama (2)**, about 80 miles (130 kilometers) southeast of the city of Calama, is also worth exploring. San Pedro de Atacama is the best town from which to visit the Atacama Desert. Several hotels serve tourists who come to San Pedro, a hardy town of mud-brick buildings on the shores of an immense, mostly dry salt lake backed by remote, snow-capped volcanoes. San Pedro is on the tourist map as the site of archaeological ruins dating back several centuries B.C.

Five miles from town is another highlight of the area: the Valley of the Moon. The valley is filled with eerie wind-carved formations of mud and salt studded with shining rocks. It is best seen at night beneath a full moon, when the spooky depression in the desert is alive with glints and reflections.

While in Bolivia, I met Felicia, a Spanish instructor spending a month in each South American country during a year's leave from her Seattle-area school. Of all her experiences in South America, she told me, the most memorable was her night hike through the Valley of the Moon with a small group of fellow visitors and their personable guide from San Pedro.

South of San Pedro de Atacama on the Argentinian border lies **Nevado Ojos del Salado (3)**, an extinct, glacier-covered volcano rising to an elevation of 22,572 feet (6,880 meters). Besides being the highest point in Chile, Ojos is the second highest point in the western hemisphere, after 22,834-foot (6,960-meter) Aconcagua just across the Chilean border from Santiago in Argentina. Ojos del Salado lies on the Chile-Argentina border, but is best climbed from Chile. Although its remote location makes the base of the mountain difficult to reach, the ascent of the peak is an excellent choice for

A wedge of glacial snow, a lift made of used truck wheels and a long steel cable equal downhill skiing at Chacaltaya ski area above La Paz, Bolivia. At more than 17,000 feet (5,180 meters) Chacaltaya is the highest ski area in the world. Credit: Scott Graham

The vertical rock *torres*, or towers, of Torres del Paine National Park jut from the surrounding grassland of southern Chile. Climbs of the towers are highly technical; backpacking in the park is superb. Credit: Mountain Travel

Grey Glacier tumbles into Grey Lake in Chile's Torres del Paine National Park. With its fjords, glaciers and spectacular mountain scenery, extreme southern Chile is not unlike Alaska and Norway far to the north. Credit: Mountain Travel

High above the Atacama Desert in the Andes of northern Chile, a hiker crosses the remote Caouena Valley. Credit: Mountain Travel

Sajama Volcano, the highest peak in Bolivia at nearly 21,500 feet (6,600 meters), provides a fine backdrop to a campsite on northern Chile's Lake Chungara in Lauca National Park. The stark lands and cool waters of Lauca are home to waterfowl, Andean condors, vicuna and other undomesticated members of the llama family. Credit: Mountain Travel

An Indian woman packs flowers to market past walls of mortarless stonework build centuries ago by her Incan ancestors. The Incas' handiwork may be viewed on day hikes and backpacking trips in the Andes surrounding the ancient Incan capital of Cuzco, Peru. Credit: Susan Graham climbers of intermediate ability who want to avoid the crowds that clog Aconcagua's slopes.

Several ski areas east of Santiago (4) are famous north of the equator for the great "summer" skiing they provide people from the northern hemisphere. The two largest areas, Portillo and Farellones, are about 70 miles (110 kilometers) east of the Chilean capital. They are generally open through the Chilean winter and into spring—from June to October—and may be reached by rental car or public transportation. Tour packages to the areas may be arranged in Santiago.

Two hundred miles (320 kilometers) south of Santiago, the **Bio Bio River (5)** flows from the Andes to the Pacific through a wilderness area of dense forests, snow-capped volcanoes and muscle-soothing hot springs. In recent years, a few adventure-travel agencies have begun offering rafting trips down the Bio Bio. Only the brave need sign up for the journey—the Bio Bio, with its unending succession of churning rapids, is known as the toughest commercially run river in the world.

The **Lake District (6)** lies south of the Bio Bio and stretches across the border into Argentina. It is far and away the most popular hiking, camping and backpacking area in Chile. In addition to numerous fine hiking trails, the area is threaded by scenic roads, while passenger ferries operate on the lakes. The area is a good place for travelers to cross into Argentina. The Argentinian ski-resort town of Bariloche lies on the eastern edge of the Lake District. On the Chilean side, the best towns from which to set off into the Lake District by foot or by vehicle are Temuco, Villarrica and Osorno.

Nearby ski areas make Temuco a popular winter resort. Temuco is the northernmost town of the Lake District, and thus nearest to Santiago.

South of Temuco lies Villarrica, on the shore of the lake of the same name. Towering above is the active, usually smoking Villarrica Volcano. Villarrica and neighboring Pucon are two of the most popular resort towns in the Lake District and both are renowned for their scenic grandeur. On some nights, flames shooting from the crater of Villarrica Volcano are reflected by the lake below. Brave souls may choose to climb the volcano, which requires snow-and-ice experience as well as nimbleness on rock and scree slopes. Climbers who reach the crater's lip will be treated to a view of the molten red bowels of the earth bubbling to the surface in the mouth of the volcano. Windsurfing is popular on Lake Villarrica, as are visits to hot springs in the area.

With a population of more than 100,000, Osorno is one of the largest cities in southern Chile. For tourists, it is little more than a transit point on the way to Lake Todos los Santos, generally regarded as the most scenic spot in the Chilean Lake District. Day tours by bus are available from Osorno to the lake, where boats take tourists out for views of the snow-capped cone of Osorno Volcano, which towers over the lake to the west.

There are several ways to visit the Lake District. Visitors whose time is limited may want to simply travel by road through the area on their way to Argentina. The Lake District can be traversed at two points by road and at other points by a combination of roads and ferries where the region's steep, narrow valleys are filled with water. The road crossings can be made in a day; the combination road-ferry crossings take two to three days, with nights spent in road- or lake-side guest houses.

Backpackers generally concentrate in Puyehue and Rosales national parks. Rosales National Park encompasses Lake Todos los Santos and Osorno Volcano. The climb of Osorno is popular among those with snow-and-ice-climbing experience. The remainder of the heavily forested park is laced with hiking trails. Puyehue National Park protects a forested region of mountains, lakes and trails north of Rosales.

For those who want to get a feel for the European flavor of the Lake District, an excellent 60-mile (100-kilometer) hike winds north to south (or vice versa) along trails and quiet back roads from village to village between Osorno and Puerto Varas. Food and some lodging are available along the way.

South of the Lake District, the city of Puerto Montt is one jumping-off point for visits to the rugged lands of southern Chile. Nearer Puerto Montt is **Chiloe Island (7)**, an enchanting land of quaint seaside fishing villages and forested hills. Ferries connect the island with the mainland. A road stretching along the east coast of Chiloe enables visitors to explore the 100-mile-long (160-kilometer-long) island by bus or rental car.

Passenger boats make the journey south along the Chilean coast from Puerto Montt to Puerto Natales. The scenery is great, but the seas can be rough and passage is not cheap. Those with sensitive stomachs or thinning wallets may wish to reach southern Chile via the new southern highway extension, or by crossing into Argentina and heading south into Patagonia by road. Both Puerto Natales and

Punta Arenas, the primary tourist destinations in southern Chile, are connected by road to southern Argentina. Regular flights also serve Punta Arenas from Santiago and Puerto Montt.

At the end of a long, narrow bay, Puerto Natales is the base for visiting **Torres del Paine National Park (8)**. The *torres*, or towers, are giant slabs of rock jutting up from the stark grasslands of southern Chile. The tallest of the towers is Cerro Paine at 7,743 feet (2,360 meters). The towers are considered by many the most stunning mountain scene in the world. The walls of the towers are so sheer they were for decades considered impossible to climb. Mount Everest fell to climbers' ropes and hardware before the summits of these towers were finally reached.

The national-park boundaries encompass the towers and a large chunk of surrounding territory that includes many glaciers and lakes. The park is populated by Andean pumas, which resemble small, female African lions, and the pumas' primary quarry, Patagonian hares and guanaco, a member of the llama family. Trails in the park take hikers alongside glaciers and lakes, along grassy valley floors and all the way around the towers. The week-long circuit of the towers is the most popular backpacking trip in the park.

Summer is the only time Torres del Paine can be visited. Even then, nighttime temperatures are low and daytime winds can be strong enough to make walking difficult. Day tours to the park can be arranged in Puerto Natales or Punta Arenas. Local buses or hired cars can be used to reach the park by those planning to stay longer than a day. If you'll be camping in the park, bring warm clothes and a good tent and sleeping bag.

Punta Arenas on the Strait of Magellan south of Puerto Natales is the southernmost city in Chile and the center for visits to Chile's share of **Patagonia (9)**. Patagonia is the name given to the large area of mountains, glaciers, rolling hills and grasslands at the southern tip of South America. It is a harsh, unforgiving land of short summers and tremendous natural beauty. Punta Arenas has grown rapidly in recent years because of the discovery of oil in the region. Today, more than 100,000 people call the city home. The most popular tourist excursion from Punta Arenas is the two-hour boat ride to Magdalena Island, the shores of which teem with tens of thousands of penguins, seals and sea lions. The island is also home to hundreds of thousands of sea birds, and the waters around the island are filled with dolphins and small whales.

Other cruises from Punta Arenas take visitors to deep fjords and to other islands in the area, including Tierra del Fuego. The island of Tierra del Fuego across the strait from Punta Arenas is the southern extremity of South America. Chile shares Tierra del Fuego with Argentina. The island is a popular place for travelers to cross from one country to another.

Easter Island (10), with its haunting, giant, carved stone heads, lies at the extreme eastern edge of Polynesia nearly 2,000 miles (3,000 kilometers) off the coast of Chile. The isolated Chilean island is served by flights from Santiago that cost about $400 round-trip. Visitors to the island can hire cars or horses to explore the ruins of the mysterious civilization that lived on the island centuries ago.

Information Sources

Two guidebooks do an excellent job of covering travel in Chile. One is *Michael's Guide to Argentina, Chile, Paraguay and Uruguay,* by Michael Shichor (Inbal Travel Information Ltd., Hunter Publishing, Inc.). Shichor's section on Chile is concise yet illuminating. The author appreciates Chile's outdoor excursions and describes many in detail. Alan Samagalski's *Chile and Easter Island: A Travel Survival Kit* (Lonely Planet Publications) is the most extensive guide to Chile published to date. Like Shichor, Samagalski appreciates and describes many of Chile's outdoor offerings.

Those planning to head for the Lake District or Torres del Paine would do well to supplement Shichor's or Samagalski's guide with *Backpacking in Chile and Argentina,* by Hilary Bradt and John Pilkington (Bradt Publications), which describes several hiking possibilities in those two countries and provides a good overview of the flora, fauna, anthropology and natural history of the southern Andes.

BOLIVIA

PARAGUAY

N

CHILE

①

②

BRAZIL

URUGUAY

③

Montevideo

Buenos
Aires

ATLANTIC
OCEAN

ARGENTINA

MILES

0   300

KILOMETERS

0   300

(Map for general location
purposes only)

⑤

Bariloche

PACIFIC
OCEAN

④

KEY

1)   Salta
2)   Iguazu Falls
3)   Aconcagua
4)   Valdes peninsula
5)   Lake District
6)   Los Glacieres National Park
7)   Tierra del Fuego

⑥ Calafate

⑦

Ushuaia

Chapter 20

Argentina

Overview

At the southern end of the South American continent, Argentina repeats many of the superb backcountry opportunities found just across its lengthy border with Chile. Along that border, western Argentina encompasses the island of Tierra del Fuego in the south, the impressive Fitzroy massif, the Alps-like Lake District, and the dry Andes in the north.

On the east coast of Argentina, the Valdes peninsula juts into the Atlantic Ocean 600 miles (1,000 kilometers) southwest of Buenos Aires, the capital of Argentina. The entire peninsula is a nature reserve that is home to a wide variety of birds and sea creatures. North of Buenos Aires on Argentina's border with Brazil, Iguazu Falls drop from a broad, flat area of tropical forest into a narrow gorge in a display of misty grandeur amid jungle foliage and brilliantly colored butterflies.

Perhaps the best news concerning Argentina's excellent backcountry possibilities is that reaching them is easy. Despite its size (Argentina is the second-largest country in Latin America after Brazil, and the eighth-largest country in the world), high-quality roads stretch to every corner of Argentina. Fleets of modern buses carry passengers along the roads, or visitors may hire rental cars. Hitchhiking is easy, too. Argentinians are eager to welcome visitors, and ask them where they're headed and what they've seen.

Internal flights make covering long distances in the country simple. In addition, Argentina is one of the few countries in Latin America where travel by train makes sense. Although train travel in the country is slower than bus travel, it is far more comfortable.

Trains run from Buenos Aires to Salta and on to Bolivia in the northwest, to Mendoza, the base city for climbing Aconcagua west of Buenos Aires, and to Bariloche in the Lake District southwest of the capital.

Argentina has a well-developed system of campgrounds throughout the country, both in its national parks and on the outskirts of many cities. Good hotels cater to visitors in every city and tourist town. Even the smallest village has some sort of accommodation for visitors.

Argentina is more Europeanized than much of the rest of Latin America. Not many Indians survived the settlement of Argentina by the Spaniards in the 1500s. The *mestizo,* or mixed, Indian-Spanish race that is prevalent in many Latin countries accounts for little of Argentina's population. Instead, most Argentinians are of pure European ancestry. Argentina's Spanish population has been augmented over the years by successive waves of immigration from other European countries, like Italy and Germany. The result has been the creation of a people mostly European in blood, yet distinctly Latin American in culture.

Despite their country's enormous potential, Argentinians have suffered almost constant economic and political problems since their country was founded. Argentina is similar to the United States in that it has a resource-rich base on which to grow. Its broad central region receives abundant rainfall and is good for crop cultivation. Other areas are ideal for cattle and sheep ranching. Oil has been discovered in Argentina, as have other mineable minerals. Nevertheless, Argentina remains politically and economically unstable. The reason, many say, is that concentration of land ownership—and hence power—has rested in the hands of only a few rich Argentinians ever since the country was settled by Spain more than four centuries ago. The rich landowners of yesteryear have given way to rich, powerful politicians and businessmen in whose hands the majority of the wealth of Argentina is concentrated today—much of it stored in European and North American banks rather than reinvested in the local economy.

The concentration of power and money in Argentina has meant that huge development loans made by North American and European banks to Argentina have found their way mostly into the pockets and bank accounts of the rich rather than into the Argentinian economy. At the close of the 1980s, Argentina owed more than $50 billion in international debt, but since most of the loan money was never invested in the country in the first place, the country had little way to pay the money back. The result was soaring inflation that culminated in food riots and civil unrest in 1989.

It is because of Argentina's tremendous natural-resource base that, despite constant corruption, the concentration of wealth in the hands of a few families and the fact that many Argentinians still live in poverty, the country has one of the highest overall standards of living in Latin America and is almost European in its modern, working infrastructure. The illiteracy rate in Argentina is less than 10 percent, and the education system is well-funded. The country's road system is the finest in Latin America. In many cities, wide boulevards are flanked by modern, high-rise buildings. In the countryside, farmers use modern techniques to plant and harvest, and farm and ranch houses are thoroughly modern. It is this infrastructure that makes a visit to Argentina comfortable and enjoyable for visitors despite the ongoing economic and political problems that plague the country.

With a population of 10 million, Buenos Aires is home to one of every three Argentinians. Buenos Aires is connected to Europe and North America by many airlines. Flights to Buenos Aires are more expensive than flights elsewhere in South America because Buenos Aires is far south. Still, flights to Buenos Aires are affordable. Since many campgrounds are available, the cost of staying in the country after leaving Buenos Aires can be almost zero. For those who camp during some or all of their stay in Argentina, a two- or three-week vacation in the country is remarkably affordable.

Geography

As you might expect of the eighth-largest country in the world, Argentina's geography is tremendously varied. Within the country's 1- million-square-mile (2.6-million-square-kilometer) territory (nearly twice the size of Alaska) are subtropical jungles, bountiful central lowlands, the highest mountain in the Americas, a 1,500-mile-long (2,400-kilometer-long) coastline, thick glaciers, almost countless rivers and the immense, mystical Patagonia region in the south.

Argentina is bordered on its long western flank by Chile, on the east by the Atlantic Ocean, and in the north by Bolivia, Paraguay, Brazil and Uruguay. Although not nearly so narrow as Chile, Argentina is narrower east to west than north to south. The country is more than 2,000 miles (3,000 kilometers) long and nearly 800 miles (1,300 kilometers) wide at its widest point.

The Andes mountains stretch the length of Argentina's western border with Chile. The highest of the Argentinian Andes is 22,834-foot (6,960-meter) Aconcagua, the highest peak in the western hemisphere. The Argentinian Andes give birth to numerous rivers that flow across the country. Many of those rivers are key transportation routes. After leaving the mountains, the rivers are fed by the runoff of the many rains that fall in the verdant central Argentinian region known as the *pampas*. The pampas is Argentina's breadbasket, where its wheat and corn crops are grown.

To the south is Patagonia, a cold, harsh land of strong winds where only hardy plants and a few determined people survive. However, the region's windswept plains, glaciers and mountains make it one of incomparable beauty.

Climate

Like its geography, Argentina's climate is quite varied. Climatically, the country stretches from the subtropics in the north, through the temperate zone that makes up the heart of Argentina, to the subarctic zone at the extreme southern end of the South American continent.

Northeastern Argentina near Iguazu Falls is junglelike in its heat and wetness. Mountainous northwestern Argentina, on the other hand, receives only enough rainfall to support cactus, other dryland vegetation, and a smattering of farms and ranches. The rainy season in Northern Argentina is during the southern-hemisphere summer, from November to March. Hence, the best time to visit northern Argentina is from May to October.

Farther south, the climate is temperate. Unless you plan to ski, late spring, summer and early fall—November to April—are best for visiting central and southern Argentina.

The subarctic region of extreme southern Argentina, like that of extreme southern Chile, is best visited in the middle of summer, when temperatures are warmest and daylight lasts up to 20 hours. Likewise, climbers venturing into the high Andes of central and southern Argentina should plan their climbs for the heart of the summer, from mid-December to mid-February.

Adventure-Travel Possibilities

Northwestern Argentina offers backpackers the opportunity to explore beautiful mountains peopled by *campesinos* who have more in common with the Andean Indians of Bolivia and Peru to the north than with their largely European countrymen to the south.

The region surrounding the colonial town of **Salta (1)** is laced with trails used by locals living in ranches and villages not connected by roads. The trails make fine walking paths for visitors as well. Wood is scarce in the dry mountains around Salta; the use of cook stoves is recommended.

Visitors to northern Argentina will not want to miss **Iguazu Falls (2)** in extreme northeastern Argentina. The falls, truly one of the wonders of the world, are described in Chapter 23.

The west-central city of Mendoza is the base from which climbers set out to climb **Aconcagua (3)**. In recent years, Argentina has promoted the mountain heavily. As a result, as many as 300 climbers at a time attempt the walk-up route on the peak's northeast ridge during the main climbing season from mid-December to mid-February. During the eight-week high season, the 14,000-foot (4,250-meter) base camp resembles a gold-mining boom town complete with canvas-tent stores and bars. The normal route on Aconcagua offers climbers the opportunity to attempt a peak said by the Argentinian tourist office to be just over 7,000 meters high (although most maps put the peak's height at 6,960 meters, or just under 23,000 feet). The route up the Polish Glacier to the top of Aconcagua offers a quiet—albeit more difficult—alternative to the busy normal route.

South of Buenos Aires along the Atlantic coast lies the broad, windy **Valdes peninsula (4)**. The entire peninsula has been set aside by the Argentinian government as a nature reserve. Visitors who time their arrival at the peninsula correctly are treated to close encounters with the hundreds of thousands of penguins, seals and sea lions that congregate on the peninsula's shores for a few months each year. The best months to visit are September to December. Dirt roads passable by two-wheel-drive vehicles allow exploration of the peninsula. Those without their own vehicle may arrange day tours of the peninsula in the nearby town of Puerto Madryn.

Directly west of the Valdes peninsula along the Chilean border lies the **Lake District (5)**. While the Chilean share of the Lake District is beautiful, the Argentinian side is truly spectacular. Lakes and forests give way to jutting, snow-covered peaks, and the entire area is good for backpacking and hiking.

The ritzy Argentinian ski-resort town of Bariloche is the jumping-off point for the most popular hike in all the Lake District—the Cerro Catedral circuit. The circuit is a three-day loop trek that begins and ends in Bariloche. The trail encircles the compact range of jutting peaks that form Bariloche's awe-inspiring backdrop to the west.

North of Bariloche, a poorly marked wilderness route takes adventurous hikers along the Chilean border in Lanin National Park between the towns of Quillen and Moquehue. The ability to use a compass is essential for this three- to five-day trek, and all supplies must be purchased ahead of time in Bariloche or some other large town.

Perhaps the most spectacular park in all of Argentina is **Los Glacieres National Park (6)** on the Chilean border several hundred miles south of the Lake District. The park contains the Moreno Glacier, which has grown in recent years while many of the world's glaciers have shrunk. The park also encompasses the Fitzroy massif, which includes jagged Mount Fitzroy and the tooth-like Cerro Torre. Together, the two vertical rock peaks form one of the most spectacular backdrops in the world. South of Los Glacieres and across the border in Chile is the equally impressive massif of the Torres del Paine.

The town of Calafate is the base for excursions to Los Glacieres park, about 50 miles (80 kilometers) away. Unlike the generally pleasant summer weather of the Lake District, the weather in Los Glacieres can be cold and harsh throughout the year. Park visitors should come prepared for rain and high winds—and for blazing sunshine as well. Visitors may use the campground at Moreno Glacier, and they may camp or stay in the hotel at the start of the trail to Mount Fitzroy and Cerro Torre. A one-day walk takes hikers to a refuge hut at the base of Fitzroy. The Fitzroy massif is often hidden by clouds and mist, even in summer. For those determined to wait for the mountains to show themselves, numerous other day and overnight hikes may be undertaken in the immediate vicinity.

Postcards of Ushuaia proclaim the town the "southernmost in the world." Literally, Ushuaia is the end of the road. It is internationally famous by virtue of its distinction as the southernmost permanently inhabited town on earth. Set on the sparkling Beagle Channel at the base of glaciers and rugged mountains nearly 1,500 miles (2,400 kilometers) south of Buenos Aires, Ushuaia is the main Argentinian outpost on **Tierra del Fuego (7)**, the island Argentina shares with Chile. Tierra del Fuego constitutes the southern tip of South America.

Ushuaia is the base for several extraordinary backcountry treks. One overnight hike takes walkers from downtown Ushuaia up a nearby valley to Martial Glacier, which is visible from town. Walking time up the well-marked trail is about ten hours and about seven to return.

The pleasant day hike to Mount Olivia, 4 miles (7 kilometers) from town, gives visitors the opportunity to view the island's red-tinged, tundra-like plants.

Seven miles (11 kilometers) from Ushuaia is Tierra del Fuego National Park, which abuts the Chilean border. The park is crisscrossed by hiking trails and is filled with wildlife.

Ushuaia also serves as a base for summer boat excursions to Wolf Island, home of a huge sea-lion colony.

Information Sources

Alan Samagalski is the author of the only guidebook exclusively on Argentina now available. Samagalski's *Argentina: A Travel Survival Kit* (Lonely Planet Publications) covers every inch of Argentina with an eye toward Argentina's many backcountry travel possibilities.

Backpacking in Chile and Argentina (Bradt Publications) contains detailed information on hikes in northern Argentina, the Lake District, Los Glacieres National Park and Tierra del Fuego.

For those who won't be spending much time in Argentina's backcountry, *Michael's Guide to Argentina, Chile, Paraguay and Uruguay* (Inbal Travel Information Ltd., Hunter Publishing, Inc.) provides useful information on overland travel in Argentina.

Chapter 21

Uruguay

Although Uruguay is one of the smallest countries in South America, it still covers an area nearly as large as the state of Nebraska. The flat, low-lying country is tucked against the Atlantic coast, with Brazil to the north and Argentina to the west and south. Much of the country is drained by the Negro River, which winds east to west across the heart of the country. Most of Uruguay's 3 million people are concentrated in large cities along the country's western and southern borders.

Uruguay is a well-developed land of farms and ranches. Although some forested land exists along its hilly northern border with Brazil, the country has no real wilderness. Hence, backcountry travel is not possible in Uruguay. Instead, visitors come to Uruguay to relax on the country's expansive, developed beaches.

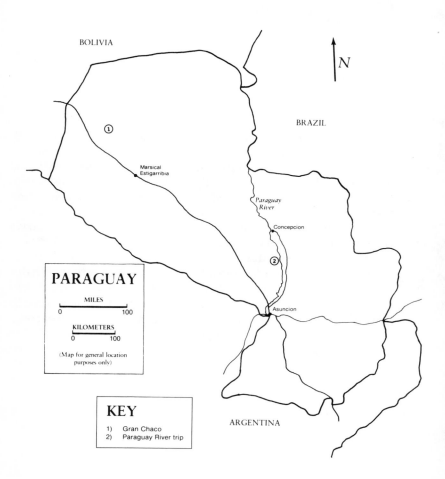

BOLIVIA

BRAZIL

①

Marsical
Estigarribia

*Paraguay
River*

Concepcion

②

PARAGUAY

MILES

0   100

KILOMETERS

0   100

(Map for general location
purposes only)

Asuncion

KEY

1)   Gran Chaco
2)   Paraguay River trip

ARGENTINA

N

Chapter 22

Paraguay

Overview

Landlocked Paraguay, wedged between Bolivia, Argentina and Brazil in south-central South America, doesn't offer much to the backcountry adventure traveler. However, the country contains one of the most adventurous road journeys in South America—the route across the sweltering western half of Paraguay to Bolivia. Visitors can also enjoy relaxing passenger-boat journeys on the Paraguay River.

Before the arrival of the Spanish in the 1500s, the region that is now Paraguay was inhabited by the Guarani Indians. Rather than conquering the peaceful Guarani, the Spaniards who settled in the area simply intermixed with the Indians. Unfortunately, Paraguay's peaceful beginning gave way, two centuries later, to the disastrous War of the Triple Alliance in the late 1800s. In that war, Paraguay fought Argentina, Brazil and Uruguay. Before the war ended in defeat for Paraguay, nine out of every ten men in Paraguay were killed.

Since the war, Paraguay has been ruled by a series of ruthless dictators. Today, the country is emerging from the isolation imposed upon it by dictator Alfredo Stroessner, who ruled the country with an iron fist for more than three decades until his overthrow in 1989. How far Paraguay will progress toward democracy under its new leadership remains to be seen. Hope was in the air, however, when I last visited the country a few weeks after the shooting had died down following the violent ouster of Stroessner.

Most of Paraguay's nearly 3 million citizens are of mixed Indian-Spanish blood, although there are sizeable numbers of pure Indians, Europeans and Asians in the country. Nearly a quarter of the country's populace lives in Asuncion, the capital of the country on the Paraguay River.

Paraguay is easy to visit if you stick to the country's main routes. Top-quality buses carry passengers in air-conditioned comfort over paved highways, and passenger boats ply the Paraguay River. The rugged journey through the vast forests of northwestern Paraguay, on the other hand, is truly an adventurous proposition.

Geography

Paraguay is a hot, humid, low-lying country. With an area of 157,000 square miles (407,000 square kilometers), it is roughly the size of California. Ninety percent of Paraguay's population lives in the eastern half of the country, which is bisected north to south by the broad Paraguay River. The eastern half of the country is given over primarily to farming and cattle grazing. The western half of the country, by comparison, is a land of dense, sweltering forests. Heat and humidity levels are high in this broad, flat region known as the Gran Chaco.

Climate

Paraguay's two overriding climatic features are heat and humidity. In the summer months, November to March, temperatures often soar to well over 100 degrees (38 degrees centigrade). When combined with high humidity levels, conditions border on the unbearable. Temperatures drop to the bearable level during winter months, but humidity remains high throughout the year. The rainy season coincides with summer; light rains generally fall from October to April. Visitors should avoid the dirt road that cuts through the Gran Chaco to Bolivia during the rainy season, when it may be impassable because of mud and washouts.

Adventure-Travel Possibilities

One of the most adventurous overland journeys in South America takes travelers from Paraguay to Bolivia, or vice versa, via the **Gran Chaco (1)**. The week-long journey involves a combination of bus travel, hitchhiking on transport trucks, and as much as 15 miles (25 kilometers) of walking between the Paraguayan and Bolivian border posts, if no vehicles are passing through the desolate strip of land between the two countries. The trip provides the only opportunity to experience the remote lands of the Chaco. Buses run the route from Asuncion, the capital of Paraguay, as far as the town of Marsical Estigarribia, in the heart of the Chaco. From there to the Bolivian border and on into Bolivia, hitchhiking is the only means of transport available to travelers.

A softer Paraguayan travel adventure is the 24-hour journey by passenger boat from **Asuncion up the Paraguay River to Concepcion (2)** through the heart of the low-lying South American tropics. From Concepcion, boats travel farther north to Bahia Negro. Some cargo boats that accept passengers even ply the river as far north as Corumba, Brazil, at the edge of the Pantanal swamp. (See the next chapter for a description of the Pantanal.)

Information Sources

Both *South America on a Shoestring* (Lonely Planet Publications), by Geoff Crowther, and *Michael's Guide to Argentina, Chile, Paraguay and Uruguay* (Inbal Travel Information Ltd., Hunter Publishing, Inc.) provide several pages of information on travel in little-visited Paraguay. Crowther provides a description of the journey across the Gran Chaco and information on passenger boats plying the Paraguay River.

BRAZIL

MILES
0 ——————— 400

KILOMETERS
0 ——————— 400

(Map for general location
purposes only)

GUYANA
VENEZUELA
SURINAME
FRENCH
GUIANA
COLOMBIA

Amazon
River
①

⑤

PERU

N

BOLIVIA
Cuiaba
②
Corumba

ATLANTIC
OCEAN

PARAGUAY
④
Sao Paolo ⑥ Rio de Janeiro

③

ARGENTINA

KEY

1) Manaus
2) Pantanal
3) Iguazu Falls
4) Itatiaia Mountain Park
5) Northeastern beaches
6) Beaches south of
    Rio de Janeiro

URUGUAY

Chapter 23

Brazil

Overview

For the adventurous traveler intent on exploring the great wilderness areas of the world, perhaps no country in Latin America holds more allure than Brazil. The vast Amazon basin of Brazil with its impenetrable jungles and native Indians is legendary.

As the international press has reported, the Amazonian rainforest, considered by many the lungs of the earth, is quickly disappearing. For now, however, huge tracts of the Amazon jungle remain untouched by chain saw and fire. Those areas may be visited by interested travelers in style aboard luxurious, air-conditioned jungle cruise boats, or by roughing it on foot or aboard small dugout canoes. Either way, those who choose to explore the Amazon basin in Brazil will be doing their bit to protect the rainforest from ultimate destruction. By spending money to visit the Amazon basin, they will be providing Brazil with a source of income from the rainforest as it exists today, rather than as hardwood lumber or as cleared land whose weak soil will support cultivation for only a year or two. And for their money, those visitors will receive a firsthand look at the largest, most verdant jungle on earth, with its riotous colors, its tangle of flora and its wealth of tropical birds and animals.

Of course, there is more to Brazil than the Amazon. There is the thundering, misty Iguazu Falls. There is the Pantanal, a vast swampland on the Bolivian border. There are beaches as long, as white, as sunny and warm as any in the world.

Altogether, Brazil is a wonderful destination for all travelers who enjoy the outdoors. Many visitors to Brazil explore the huge country—it is the fifth largest in the world—for months at a time. However, for those whose time is limited, a comfortable visit to the Amazon jungle, the Pantanal and Iguazu Falls could easily be accomplished in as little as three weeks. Domestic flights are inexpensive in Brazil, so the vast distances between sites in the country can be covered quickly and affordably. Brazil's domestic airlines offer air passes good for unlimited flights on their routes for either two or three weeks. The passes must be purchased outside the country. At less than $400 for a three-week pass, they are excellent value. For those with more time and less money, Brazil's buses are cheap, fast and convenient.

Despite all the pleasure and excitement of a trip to Brazil, it is impossible to visit the country without learning something of the daunting problems the country faces—problems that are ultimately the root cause of the intensifying destruction of Brazil's one great resource, the Amazon rainforest. Those problems will become apparent to you as soon as you exchange money upon your arrival in the country. For the few dollars or traveler's checks you exchange, you'll receive some thousands or millions of *cruzeiros, cruzados, novo cruzados* or whatever the latest currency is named in Brazil. The reason? Runaway inflation brought on by Brazil's ongoing economic crisis.

The economic crisis in Brazil is the result of years of wanton borrowing—often with the encouragement of international lending agencies—and unregulated spending by the Brazilian government that has left the country more than $100 billion in debt to North American and European banks.

The country's economic crisis is exacerbated by the explosive population growth that has been occurring in Brazil since the turn of the century. In 1900, there were 17 million people living in Brazil. Today, the number is estimated at close to 150 million. More than 50 percent of the population of South America lives in Brazil. Far too great a percentage of that number lives in the sprawling, squalid, inhuman shantytowns that ring every large Brazilian city.

There has long been a large gap between the rich and the poor in Brazil, and it is growing ever larger. Today, 1 percent of the population of Brazil controls half the country's wealth. Brazil's middle class, which grew steadily in earlier, better times, is fast disappearing. Hopelessness and desperation are pervasive among the country's have-nots, more than half of whom are school-age children. There is little money for education; illiteracy is on the rise; children are on the streets. They roam the poor neighborhoods of

Brazil's large cities in packs, swarming over unsuspecting pedestrians, grabbing wallets, purses and jewelry.

Brazil's economic and population crises threaten more than just children. The Brazilian government in recent years has encouraged the ever-faster clearing of the rainforest to generate quick income from the forest's valuable hardwoods and to open up new settlement areas for the country's burgeoning population. Today, so much of the forest is falling to loggers' chain saws and to settlers' fires that the remaining forest may not last into the next century. The international outcry to save the rainforest has been loud. You can add your own voice—and dollars—to the outcry by visiting Brazil and the rainforest.

Despite the dire economic conditions in Brazil, you'll enjoy your visit to the country. Despite the problems they face, Brazilians enjoy sharing their tropical, sunny, wildly exotic homeland with visitors.

Your visit to Brazil will also be remarkably affordable. Sad though it is, the inflation hurting Brazil's poor makes the country inexpensive for visitors. In addition, the prices of plane flights from North America and Europe to Rio and elsewhere in Brazil, once the most expensive destinations in South America, have dropped a great deal in recent years.

The primary language in Brazil is Portuguese because the country was colonized by Portugal rather than Spain. Many Brazilians speak English, however, and visitors who speak Spanish are often understood by Brazilians since Spanish and Portuguese are similar.

Geography

Brazil lies on the east coast of the South American continent. Its land mass of 3.3 million square miles (8.5 million square kilometers) makes it almost as large as the United States. Brazil's coastline stretches for nearly 5,000 miles (8,000 kilometers) along the Atlantic Ocean. Inland, the country shares its border with every other country in South America except Chile and Ecuador.

The Amazon River and the huge area of Brazil it drains are the chief distinguishing features of northern Brazil. The Amazon grows from thousands of tributary streams and rivers flowing from the flanks of the Andes Mountains of Bolivia, Peru, Ecuador and Colombia. The Amazon flows east across northern Brazil, just south of the equator. The immense Amazon basin covers 60 percent of the country, yet is home to only 4 percent of the country's people.

Southwestern Brazil is a sparsely populated land of savanna and swamp. In far western Brazil on the banks of the Paraguay River lie the Pantanal swamps. South of the Pantanal is Iguazu Falls. Southeastern Brazil is the major industrial and agricultural area of the country. Most of the population of Brazil is concentrated in the huge cities of southeastern Brazil, including Sao Paulo with 13 million people, Rio de Janeiro with 10 million, and Belo Horizonte with nearly 3 million.

Much of the southern coast of Brazil is lined by steep, green, thickly forested mountains reaching nearly 10,000 feet (3,000 meters) in elevation. Hiking trails wind through the mountains, which serve as a scenic backdrop to the beaches of the south coast.

Climate

As you would expect of a country cut by the equator, the prevailing climate in Brazil is hot and humid. Only in extreme southern Brazil does the climate begin to shift from tropical to temperate. There, temperatures sometimes drop as low as freezing.

As in all tropical countries, temperatures in Brazil are fairly constant. Rain is likely in the heart of the Amazon basin throughout the year. Farther south, the rainy season runs roughly from January or February to June or July. If possible, plan to visit the Pantanal during the middle of the July-to-December dry season, when much of the swamplands are dry and access to the region and its wildlife by four-wheel-drive vehicle is possible on seasonal roads.

Adventure-Travel Possibilities

Most visitors use **Manaus (1)**, on the banks of the Amazon 1,000 miles (1,600 kilometers) upstream from the Atlantic Ocean, as a base from which to explore the jungle. Manaus is the largest city on the Amazon, with a population of more than half-a-million people. It is also a major international tourist destination. Visitors may book any sort of jungle adventure they wish with the many tour agencies in Manaus, or through adventure-travel agencies in North America and Europe before they leave home. Most popular are stays at jungle lodges on tributaries of the Amazon near Manaus. From these lodges, visitors may take day or overnight trips deeper into the jungle. Also popular are group tours deep into the jungle by hired dugout canoe. Tour members generally camp or stay in Indian villages along their route. Travel by dugout canoe is rough—seating can be cramped, the sun can be hot, and the rains steady. Despite such drawbacks, tours by dugout enable visitors to experience the way the Indians of the Amazon basin live and travel. In addition, tours by canoe generally visit remote areas of the jungle where more wildlife and unspoiled plant life is seen than near jungle lodges. Note, however, that the Manaus area is so populated that only lengthy tours—eight to ten days—venture far enough from the city to give participants a true taste of the unspoiled rainforest. Prices range from more than $100 a day to stay at the best jungle lodges to $30 or $40 a day on group backcountry tours by dugout canoe.

In addition to being the best base in Brazil for exploring the Amazon rainforest, Manaus is also a good point from which to travel up or down the Amazon River. Although Manaus is far from the sea, the Amazon is so deep that ocean-going ships regularly visit the city. The Amazon, which carries 15 times more water than the Mississippi River, is 5 miles (8 kilometers) wide at Manaus. From the Manaus port, river boats that accept passengers as well as cargo travel upstream to the borders of Colombia and Peru, and downstream all the way to Belem at the Amazon's mouth. Combination cargo-passenger boats also ply some of the tributaries of the Amazon from Manaus to remote towns and villages in the region.

If you plan to voyage by river boat from Manaus, arrive prepared. Even if you travel first class, you may need mosquito netting and your own bedding. No matter what class you travel, you'll need bug repellent, your own food, and plenty of bottled water or the ability to purify with iodine or filter the water available on board.

The **Pantanal (2)** region of western Brazil has become increasingly popular with nature lovers in recent years. The swamps and marshes of the Pantanal are formed by the waters of the Paraguay River, which overflow the river's banks during the rainy season, covering a huge area of low-lying land. The area is administered by the Brazilian national-park system and is considered one of the greatest wildlife reserves in the world. Hundreds of bird species live in the Pantanal, along with the elusive ocelot, the jaguar, various monkey species, deer, wild boars, crocodiles, anacondas, anteaters, and herds of capybara, the largest member of the rodent family. Many of these species are also found in the Amazon basin, but they can be viewed more easily in the Pantanal because the area isn't as thickly covered with foliage as the Amazon jungle.

As the waters of the Paraguay River recede with the onset of the dry season, the wildlife of the Pantanal is drawn ever closer to remaining water holes. Meanwhile, the now-dry marshlands support the weight of four-wheel-drive vehicles, which carry visitors from towns near the Pantanal deep into the area to view the wildlife. The result is an affordable wildlife-viewing safari matched in scope and variety only by safaris in East Africa. Tours of the Pantanal that include transportation, meals and camping facilities may be arranged in the towns of Corumba, south of the Pantanal, and Cuiaba, north of the Pantanal, for as little as $15 to $20 a day. Both Corumba and Cuiaba are served by Brazil's domestic airlines.

During the rainy season, the only Pantanal tours available are by boat up and down the Paraguay River. Even then, the flowers, water birds, crocodiles and iguanas you'll see make a visit worthwhile.

South of the Pantanal are the incomparable **Iguazu Falls (3)**, one of the world's greatest natural wonders. "Poor Niagara," Eleanor Roosevelt is reported to have said when she first viewed Iguazu Falls. Her sentiment is probably shared by most North Americans who visit the falls, located on the border of Brazil and Argentina near Paraguay.

The falls are formed by the Iguazu River as it spreads to a width of nearly 3 miles (5 kilometers) and tumbles off a huge, horseshoe-shaped cliff in a series of falls 300 feet (90 meters) high. Nearly half-a-million gallons (1.9 million liters) of water pour off the falls every second in a thunderous roar audible for miles. Mist from the falls rises high in the air, where magnificent, undulating rainbows appear. The area around the falls is a luxuriant jungle filled with flowers and butterflies. Nature trails wind through the jungle growth to numerous observation points above and below the falls, each seemingly more breathtaking than the last.

Visiting Iguazu Falls, though exciting, is by no means adventurous. More than 2 million tourists visit the falls each year. Paved roads lead to both sides of the falls, and paved trails with handrails and stairways at steep points go on from there. Still, the falls are a magnificent sight that should be included in any visit to Brazil, Argentina or Paraguay if time permits.

Itatiaia Mountain Park (4), just off the main highway between Rio de Janeiro and Sao Paolo in southeastern Brazil, is a verdant wonderland of mountains, streams and waterfalls threaded by a network of trails for hikers and backpackers.

Although the famous beaches of Rio de Janeiro are beautiful, they're also crowded. If you'd like to relax on a tranquil beach, head north or south from Rio along the ocean. Brazil's entire coast is lined with spectacular beaches. The most famous are the **beaches of northeastern Brazil (5)**, near the cities of Natal and Fortaleza. The **beaches south of Rio toward Sao Paolo (6)**, although more crowded, are also superb. Two islands just off this section of coast, Ilha Grande and Ihlabela, are popular with outdoors enthusiasts. Of the two, Ihla Grande is the less developed. Camping is possible along the island's quiet beaches, and hiking trails wind along the island's mountainous spine. Ihlabela is known for its tremendous natural beauty. It is more developed than Ihla Grande, but still has sections of backcountry that can be reached only on foot.

Information Sources

For outdoors enthusiasts, the best guide to Brazil available today is *Backcountry Brazil* (Bradt Publications) by Alex Bradbury, which provides good general coverage of the Pantanal and Amazonia as well as detailed descriptions of several hikes along the Brazilian coast. *Michael's Guide to Brazil,* by Michael Shichor (Inbal Travel Information Ltd., Hunter Publishing, Inc.) does a fine job of describing the many outdoor-travel possibilities awaiting visitors in Brazil. Shichor provides information on Brazil's cities as well, but his emphasis is on the outdoors.

Lonely Planet Publications' *Brazil: A Travel Survival Kit* follows the mold of other Lonely Planet "travel survival kits," and directs visitors to many adventures in the Brazilian backcountry. The book even includes information on rock climbing in and near Rio de Janeiro.

The four authors of *Brazil: The Real Guide* (Prentice Hall Press) provides much detail about lodging and restaurants for independent travelers to Brazil, as well as some general information on backcountry activities in the country.

VENEZUELA

ATLANTIC
OCEAN

N

Georgetown

GUYANA

SURINAME

FRENCH
GUIANA

BRAZIL

THE GUIANAS

MILES

0   120

KILOMETERS

0   120

(Map for general location
purposes only)

Chapter 24

The Guianas

Guyana, Suriname and French Guiana reflect the small role northern Europe played in colonizing the South American continent. As Spain and Portugal divided most of the continent between themselves, England, Holland and France established beachheads on the sodden, jungled northern coast of the continent. The three countries they founded remain little developed to this day. Only the coastlines of the three countries are developed. Inland, the countries remain the realm of Indians living deep in the virgin jungles and rainforests of the Guianas, which lie just north of the equator and the immense Amazon basin.

If low-lying Uruguay is the only country in South America not worth exploring by adventure travelers because it is so well-developed, then Guyana, Suriname (formerly Dutch Guiana) and French Guiana represent the other extreme. The countries are little visited, even though they lie just across the Gulf of Mexico from the United States. Torrential rains continue unabated virtually year-round in the countries, which are noted as well for their unrelenting heat and humidity. Since virtually no roads lead inland from the coastal farmlands of the Guianas, it is impossible for short-term visitors to explore the vast jungles and rain-forested highlands of the three small countries, of which next to nothing has been written in guidebooks.

Of the three countries, Guyana is the most developed. It has one rough road that cuts south nearly as far as the Brazilian border. Unfortunately, tourism has been discouraged in Guyana since the mass suicide in 1979 of the Rev. Jim Jones and hundreds of his North American followers, who were living on a fanatical religious commune in the country.

If your time is short, you're well advised to give the Guianas a miss, no matter how much you itch to explore virgin territory. On the other hand, with all the difficulties facing anyone with enough time and desire to explore the isolated jungles and highlands of the region, the Guianas may offer Latin America's ultimate travel adventure.

Adventure Travel Activities by Country

(As described in this book)

	Day Hiking	Backpacking/Trekking	Camping	Mountain Climbing	Snorkeling/Diving	Sea Kayaking	Windsurfing	River rafting/Kayaking	River Boat Trips	Jungle Trips	Overland Public Transportation Trips
Argentina	x	x	x	x							
Belize	x		x		x	x	x			x	
Bolivia	x	x	x	x					x		x
Brazil	x	x	x		x				x	x	
Caribbean	x	x	x	x	x	x	x			x	
Chile	x	x	x	x				x			
Colombia	x	x	x	x	x					x	
Costa Rica	x	x	x	x	x					x	
Ecuador	x	x	x	x	x				x	x	
Guatemala	x	x	x	x							
Honduras	x	x	x	x	x					x	
Mexico	x	x	x	x	x	x	x			x	
Nicaragua	x										
Panama	x	x	x	x						x	
Paraguay									x		x
Peru	x	x	x	x				x	x	x	
Venezuala	x	x	x	x	x				x	x	

Index

(boldface indicates primary listing)

ABOUT THE AUTHOR

Scott Graham was raised in the mountains of southwestern Colorado. He has lived in Spain and traveled extensively in Europe, Africa, Asia and Latin America. He is the author of *Backpacking and Camping in the Developing World*, published by Wilderness Press in 1988. A journalist by degree, and business and travel writer by profession, Graham lives in New Mexico's Manzano Mountains with his wife, Susan.